Hreha

ATM, Volume III

ISBN 0-13-784182-5

9 780137 841820

90000

Prentice Hall Series In
Advanced Communications Technologies

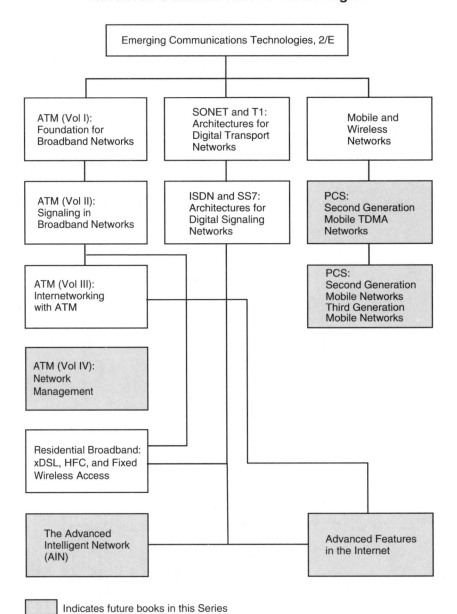

Emerging Communications Technologies, 2/E

ATM (Vol I):
Foundation for
Broadband Networks

SONET and T1:
Architectures for
Digital Transport
Networks

Mobile and
Wireless
Networks

ATM (Vol II):
Signaling in
Broadband Networks

ISDN and SS7:
Architectures for
Digital Signaling
Networks

PCS:
Second Generation
Mobile TDMA
Networks

ATM (Vol III):
Internetworking
with ATM

PCS:
Second Generation
Mobile Networks
Third Generation
Mobile Networks

ATM (Vol IV):
Network
Management

Residential Broadband:
xDSL, HFC, and Fixed
Wireless Access

The Advanced
Intelligent Network
(AIN)

Advanced Features
in the Internet

Indicates future books in this Series

ATM, Volume III
INTERNETWORKING
WITH ATM

UYLESS BLACK

To join a Prentice Hall PTR Internet mailing list, point to:
http://www.prenhall.com/mail_lists/

Prentice Hall PTR
Upper Saddle River, New Jersey 07458

Library of Congress Cataloging-in-Publication Data

Black, Uyless D.
   ATM—Vol.III: Internetworking with ATM / Uyless Black.
     p. cm.
   Includes bibliographical references and index.
   ISBN 0–13–784182–5
   1. Asynchronous transfer mode. 2. Broadband communication
systems. I Title.
   TK5105.35.B53 1995
   621.382—dc20   95–5961
                                             CIP

Acquisitions editor: Mary Franz
Cover designer: Scott Weiss
Cover design director: Jerry Votta
Manufacturing manager: Alexis R. Heydt
Marketing manager: Miles Williams
Compositor/Production services: Pine Tree Composition, Inc.

 Published by Prentice Hall PTR
Prentice-Hall, Inc.
A Simon & Schuster Company
Upper Saddle River, New Jersey 07458

Prentice Hall books are widely-used by corporations and government agencies for training, marketing, and resale.

The publisher offers discounts on this book when ordered in bulk quantities. For more information contact:

      Corporate Sales Department
      Phone: 800–382–3419
      Fax: 201–236–7141
      E-mail: corpsales@prenhall.com

      Or write:

      Prentice Hall PTR
      Corp. Sales Dept.
      One Lake Street
      Upper Saddle River, New Jersey 07458

Printed in the United States of America
10 9 8 7 6 5 4 3 2

ISBN: 0-13-784182-5

Prentice-Hall International (UK) Limited, *London*
Prentice-Hall of Australia Pty. Limited, *Sydney*
Prentice-Hall Canada Inc., *Toronto*
Prentice-Hall Hispanoamericana, S.A., *Mexico*
Prentice-Hall of India Private Limited, *New Delhi*
Prentice-Hall of Japan, Inc., *Tokyo*
Simon & Schuster Asia Pte. Ltd., *Singapore*
Editora Prentice-Hall do Brasil, Ltda., *Rio de Janeiro*

The effective internetworking of computers, switches, routers, and bridges requires a great deal of cooperative interaction between these machines. In a sense, they must have some type of social structure in order for the networks that they create to be able to transport information. Since they may be in different geographical areas, perhaps far-apart from each other, a process called path discovery is executed between them in order to build an efficient route between the machines. Furthermore, the route, once learned, must be retained, and if necessary, updated to reflect changing conditions in the system.

In conducting research for the books in this series, and as part of my interest in nature, I have noticed the similarities of computer networks' behavior to that of creatures in the natural world. For this book, I have chosen the common ant as an analogy to computer networking.

Like computer networks, the ant's "social" behavior in building and maintaining their networks of colonies and nests is quite complex, one of the most elaborate in the insect world. But the scientists who study ants are not certain how the ants decide how to build (or abandon) some of these networks. Indeed, the communications between ants occurs through a perplexing combination of smell, taste, touch, and antennae movement.

One of the most fascinating aspects of computer networking is route discovery, and I have wondered how the ant performs this feat—how they know where their home base is, after wondering about in their foraging labors. Generally, the ant finds its way, largely by environmental clues. But on occasion, it operates like a first-generation route discovery protocol; not very efficient. For example, some ants use a process called light-compass orientation, and take their clues from the sun's angle to them. Try placing a box on top of an ant that is walking about. If the box is left over the ant for say an hour, and then removed, the ant will strike out in a different direction from its original course, by an angle equal to the number of degrees the sun moved during the ant's confinement. Well, not too impressive. Maybe something like looping packets through a network again-and-again.

One of the most remarkable attributes of ants is their prodigious strength. Some can lift a stone some 60 times their own weight. That impressive fact led me to use them for the cover of this book, symbolized by their carting-around Frame Relay, ATM, and other networks.

The ant is quite efficient; it does not waste much time hauling non-productive things to its colony. So, even though virtual networks are part of the subject matter of this book, I chose not to show this term on the cover. After all, no self-respecting ant would waste its time transporting something that doesn't exist.

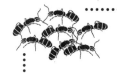

Contents

Preface

This book is one in a collection of books titled Advanced Communications Technologies. It is also a companion to two Asynchronous Transfer Mode (ATM) books in this series, volumes I and II, titled *ATM: Foundation for Broadband Networks,* and *ATM: Signaling in Broadband Networks,* respectively.

This volume deals with a major issue in the industry: integrating the ATM technology into existing systems. The approach taken is called internetworking (or interworking): connecting ATM networks to existing systems. In so far as possible, the internetworking operations makes the presence of ATM transparent to the existing systems.

If ATM is to be successful, prominent technologies must be supported by ATM, or integrated into the ATM technology. Several of these technologies are discussed in this book. They are: (a) Frame Relay, (b) Ethernet and Token Ring local area networks, and (c) Internet Protocol (IP)-based internets and intranets.

Many issues surrounding the subject of ATM internetworking must be resolved, such as migration plans, deployment schedules, and acquisition decisions. Moreover, the tradeoffs of ATM vs. Fast Ethernet, and ATM vs. IPv6 (IP, version 6) are far from settled. In many network situations, these technologies provide attractive alternatives to ATM.

However, the majority of the technical issues pertaining to the internetworking of ATM to Frame Relay, Ethernet, Token Ring, and IP have been resolved, due to the work of the ATM Forum, the Frame Relay

Forum, several Internet Task Forces, and some of the formal standards bodies. It is this subject that this book addresses.

I hope you find this information useful, and this book a welcome addition to your library. I can be reached at:

102732.3535@compuserve.com.

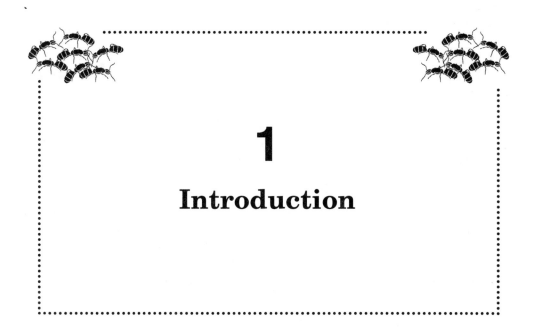

1

Introduction

This chapter introduces ATM internetworking and describes why having ATM as part of an internetworking operation can provide benefits to an organization. Key internetworking concepts are explained, and ATM is compared to the major systems with which it may interwork.

REASONS FOR INTERNETWORKING

Internetworking is the sharing of computer resources by connecting the computers through a number of data communications networks. The networks can be public or private networks; they can be local or wide area networks. Perhaps the most common shared resources are the computing cycles on a machine and software, typically on some type of "server" computer. Common databases are also shared through internetworking.

Reasons for Internetworking with ATM

As just stated, internetworking allows the users of different networks to exchange information with each other. For this book, one of the networks is an ATM system. One might ask why an organization would want to add ATM to the internetworking picture.

First, the deployment of ATM to support other networks is consistent with the trend toward increased use of ATM in multiservice (voice, data, video) networks. Second, carriers and service providers can accommodate the continuing growth of Frame Relay and LAN services (as two examples) and the more modest growth of ATM services. Third, carriers and service providers can support the trend toward service consolidation at the customer premises. Fourth, ATM offers high-speed trunks that permit the negotiation of quality of service (QOS) features, such as delay, throughput, and peak burst rate. These features are not supported by most other technologies.

Internetworking also permits the distribution of resources—an important element in load leveling and backup operations. Indeed, distributed processing is made possible through internetworking.

TERMS AND DEFINITIONS

Internetworking and Interworking

The term *internetworking (or interworking) unit (IWU)* is used to describe a machine that performs relaying functions between networks. Other terms are explained shortly.[1]

The networks are often called *subnetworks*. The term does not mean that they provide fewer functions than a conventional network. Rather, it means that the subnetworks contribute to the overall operations for internetworking. Stated another way, subnetworks comprise an internetwork or an internet.

An internetworking unit is designed to remain transparent to the end user application. Typically, the end user application resides in the host machines connected to the networks; rarely are user applications placed in the IWU. This approach is attractive from several standpoints. First, the IWU need not burden itself with application layer protocols. Since they are not invoked at the IWU, the IWU can dedicate itself to fewer tasks, such as managing the traffic between networks. It is not concerned with application layer functions such as database access, electronic mail, and file management.

---

[1]The terms internetworking and interworking are used to describe the relaying of traffic between networks. Some specifications use one term; other specifications use the other. They are synonymous and this book uses both terms.

L_2 and L_3 Protocol Data Units (PDUs)

This book uses the notation L_2 to describe a layer 2 protocol, also known as a data link layer protocol. The notation L_3 describes a layer 3 protocol operating at the network layer. The network layer is also called the internetwork(ing) layer in many of the Internet and ATM Forum specifications.

Also, the term *PDU* (for protocol data unit) describes the unit of traffic sent across the communications link. Some of the standards and specifications discussed in this book use other terms in place of PDU, such as packet, message, or frame.

This book equates a *frame* to either a L_1 (physical layer) PDU or a L_2 PDU. It equates a *datagram* to a connectionless L_3 PDU, and a *packet* to a connection-oriented L_3 PDU.

The term *message* is used generally to describe any type of PDU. The term *cell* is used exclusively for the ATM PDU. The term *segment* will describe a L_4 PDU (notably a TCP or UDP segment). A *fragment* will describe any type of PDU that has been broken up into smaller PDUs.

Addresses[2] and Virtual Circuit Identifiers

Whether a PDU is a cell, datagram, or frame, it must have some type of an identifier in its header in order for the IWU to relay it to the correct destination. This identifier also distinguishes the PDU from PDUs associated with different end-to-end data flows.

Two types of identifiers are used in most computer-based networks: an address and a virtual circuit identifier (ID). An address has (or can be made to have) geographical significance and hence is inherently routable. Examples are a telephone number (area code and exchange code) and the IP address (a network and subnetwork identifier). Virtual circuit IDs are simply labels attached to the PDU to uniquely identify one PDU from another. The virtual circuit ID is not inherently routable, but the common practice is to construct routing tables (usually called cross-connect tables) in the IWU for the purpose of using the virtual circuit ID for just that—routing.

Why have two identifiers? Simply put, it comes down to a difference in opinion on how to identify traffic. It is also a result of how the industry and different network technologies evolved over the past twenty-five years.

---

[2]Appendix B provides a description of the addresses commonly used in the industry.

Routing and Switching

Currently in vogue is the debate on the difference between routing and switching. Here are some definitions:

- Routing is performed in software while switching is performed in hardware.
- Routing uses addresses while switching uses virtual circuit IDs.

These definitions are clouded by two terms: IP switching and tag switching. Vendors/operators vary on their definitions of these two terms.

IP switching is the use of fast processors to relay IP datagrams and uses a mix of hardware and software, but it is designed to reduce the latency in processing the IP datagram through the IWU. Tag switching uses a label to assist in processing the PDU at the IWU. Indeed, the label may be a virtual circuit ID. Therefore, in IP-based systems, tag switching is a form of IP switching.

Specific Terms for the Virtual Circuit ID

A rose by any other name is still a rose and a virtual circuit ID by any other name is still a virtual circuit ID. Here are the terms used in the industry:

- ATM   Virtual path ID (VPI)/virtual channel ID (VCI)
- Frame Relay   Data link connection ID (DLCI)
- X.25   Logical channel number (LCI)

Correlating Addresses and Virtual Circuit IDs

In several of the networks discussed in this book, both addressing and virtual circuit IDs are used. A common practice in ATM is to set up a connection first, by using a source and destination address; second, during the connection setup process, associating these addresses with a VPI/VCI; and third, constructing appropriate entries in the cross-connect table. Thereafter, high-speed switching can take place by using the short VPI/VCI instead of a lengthy, cumbersome address.

ATM INTERNETWORKING EXAMPLES

Figure 1–1 shows the relationship of the an ATM internetworking interface to other interfaces and protocols. All these technologies, as well

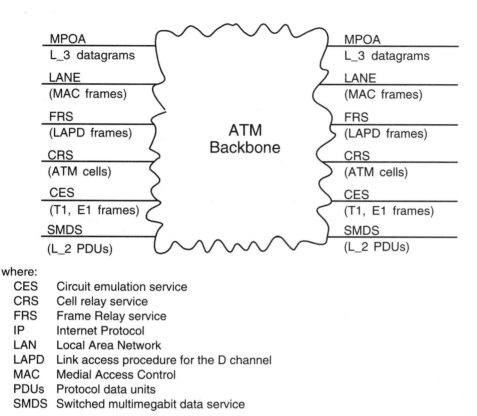

where:

CES	Circuit emulation service
CRS	Cell relay service
FRS	Frame Relay service
IP	Internet Protocol
LAN	Local Area Network
LAPD	Link access procedure for the D channel
MAC	Medial Access Control
PDUs	Protocol data units
SMDS	Switched multimegabit data service

Figure 1–1   ATM internetworking examples.

as ATM, provide for the user-to-network interface, which is called either a UNI, or a subscriber-to-network (SNI).[3]

Traffic can be submitted to a network in ATM cells, E1/T1 frames, LAN frames, Frame Relay frames, or SMDS (PDUs). This traffic is sent across the interface in the form of (1) ATM cells over ATM connections; (2) E1/T1 frames (CES), which are encapsulated into AAL type 1 PDUs; (3) Frame Relay frames, which are encapsulated into AAL type 5 PDUs and mapped into ATM cells; (4) SMDS PDUs, which are encapsulated into AAL type 3/4 PDUs and mapped into ATM cells, or LAN frames which are encapsulated into AAL5 PDUs and ATM cells. The LAN frames typically carry IP or IPX datagrams.

The ATM backbone has considerable functionality. It contains inter-working units, which transmit and receive traffic from different systems.

---

[3]Internetworking ATM and T1 (CES) and ATM and SMDS are covered in Volume I of this series.

The term gateway is sometimes used to describe this function. This aspect of ATM is in keeping with ATM's design to support multiservice traffic.

Frame Relay frames can be encapsulated into AAL type 5 PDUs and the Frame Relay data link connection identifier (DLCI) is sent through the networks and translated at the receiving Frame Relay interface. Alternately, if frames are mapped to the ATM layer, a DLCI must be translated into an ATM VPI/VCI. Finally, SMDS PDUs can be encapsulated into AAL type 3/4 PDUs.

Through a process called LAN Emulation (LANE), ATM can act as a backbone to multiple LANs. In effect, the ATM nodes emulate bridges because they process LAN frames and the MAC addresses in the frames. Finally, with Multiprotocol Over ATM (MPOA) network layer traffic (IP, IPX) can be passed to/from the ATM backbone.

COMPARISON OF ATM AND FRAME RELAY

While we assume that the reader is familiar with Frame Relay and ATM operations, it is a good idea to pause briefly and compare some of the major attributes of these two technologies. Table 1–1 makes such a comparison. It consists of three columns: the first column is labeled attribute, which describes the characteristics (attributes) of the technology in a short phrase; the next two columns, labeled Frame Relay and ATM, describe how these technologies use or do not use the attribute. Further comparisons for these technologies is available in the flagship book for this series, *Emerging Communications Technologies,* second edition.

The ATM and Frame Relay Headers

Figure 1–2 illustrates the headers for Frame Relay and ATM. They are more alike than different, in that each contains a virtual circuit id, which is called the data link connection identifier (DLCI) in Frame Relay and the virtual path identifier/virtual channel identifier (VPI/VCI) in ATM. Both contain bits to allow the traffic to be tagged in the event of problems; for Frame Relay this is called the discard eligibility (DE) bit and for ATM it is called cell loss priority (CLP).

Both technologies provide for congestion notification. For Frame Relay this feature is provided in the forward explicit congestion notification (FECN) and the backward explicit congestion notification (BECN) bits. For ATM, this feature is provided in the bits residing in the payload type identifier (PTI), which is known generically as congestion notifica-

Table 1–1   Major Attributes of Frame Relay and ATM

Attribute	Frame Relay	ATM
Application support?	Asynchronous data (with voice gaining in use [but not designed for voice])	Asynchronous, synchronous voice, video, data
Connection mode?	Connection-oriented	Connection-oriented
Congestion management?	Yes, congestion notification, traffic tagging (DE bit), and possible traffic discard	Yes, congestion notification, traffic tagging (CLP bit), and possible traffic discard
Method of identifying traffic?	Virtual circuit id: the DLCI	Virtual circuit id: The VPI/VCI
PVCs?	Yes	Yes
SVCs (connections on demand)?	Yes	Yes
Congestion notification technique?	The FECN and BECN bits	The CN bits in the PTI field
Traffic tagging technique?	The discard eligibility (DE) bit	The cell loss priority (CLP) bit
LAN or WAN technology?	WAN based	Either
PDU size?	Variable (PDU is called a frame)	Fixed at 53 bytes (PDU is called a cell)
Sequencing of traffic?	No	Cell header, no; for AAL payload, depends on AAL type
ACKs/NAKs retransmissions?	No	Only for signaling traffic on SVCs

BECN	Backward explicit congestion notification
CLP	Cell loss priority
DE	Discard eligibility
DLCI	Data link connection identifier
FECN	Forward explicit congestion notification
LAN	Local area network
PDU	Protocol data unit
SVC	Switched virtual call
VCI	Virtual channel identifier
VPI	Virtual path identifier
WAN	Wide area network

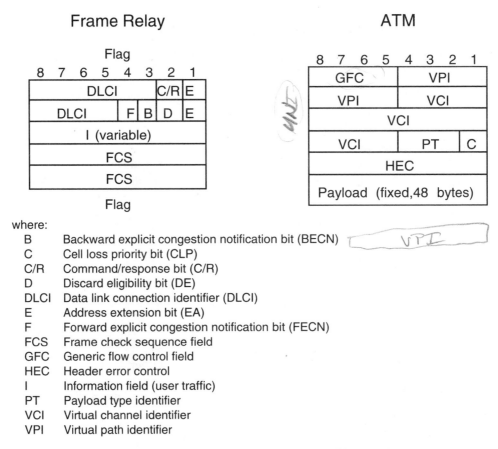

Figure 1–2   The Frame Relay and ATM headers.

tion. ATM provides no mechanism for identifying forward or backward congestion notification with these bits.

Figure 1–2 provides other information that is pertinent to this discussion. Notice that the Frame Relay header is actually embedded into another protocol data unit (PDU), which is considered part of the overall Frame Relay header and trailer (protocol control information [PCI]). This PCI is nothing more than flags that are used to delineate the beginning and ending of traffic, and the frame check sequence field (FCS) is used to perform an error check at the receiver to determine if the information between the flags were damaged while in transit.

In contrast, ATM does not contain flag-type fields and its error checking is performed with the fifth byte of the header, called the header error correction (HEC) field. This field error corrects any one-bit error in the header and will detect most others. But it operates differently from the Frame Relay FCS field in that it performs forward error correction. The Frame Relay FCS only does error detection and not error correction.

COMPARISON OF ATM AND LAN TECHNOLOGIES

While we also assume that the reader is somewhat familiar with LAN and ATM operations, it is a good idea to pause briefly and compare some of the major attributes of these technologies. Table 1–2 makes such a comparison. It consists of four columns: The first column is labeled attribute and describes the characteristics (attributes) of the technology in a short phrase; the next four columns, labeled Ethernet, IEEE 802.3, IEEE 802.5, and ATM, describe how these technologies use or do not use the attribute. For ease of reference, I include the ATM information that is also in Table 1–1.

One key concept to note in this table is that LANs are connectionless and ATM is connection-oriented. LANs do not create connections with each other; they send and receive traffic without regard to a connection setup. In contrast, ATM is connection-oriented and sets up virtual circuits before sending traffic.

Additionally, ATM nodes are identified with an ATM address, and LAN nodes are identified with the 48-bit MAC address. This aspect—different addresses—means an IWU must be able to map or correlate these addresses in an ATM/LAN interworking operation. This operation is called address resolution and is one of the principal subjects of this book. It is introduced in Chapter 2, and explained further in sebsequent chapters.

Notice also that LANs do not provide much in the way of value-added services, such as sequencing, congestion notifications, and so on; whereas, ATM provides for a number of these services.

Also, notice the attribute "Encapsulation header." It too is a major part of this book and is explained in Chapter 2.

COMPARISON OF ATM AND IP

To complete the comparisons of the technologies discussed in this book, Table 1–3 compares the major features of IP and ATM. The ATM column in Tables 1–1 and 1–2 is repeated for the convenience of the reader.

Once again, the different technologies use different identifiers ("method of identifying traffic") and different encapsulation headers ("Encapsulation header"). These features are also explained in Chapter 2.

Table 1–2   Comparisons of ATM and LAN Technologies

Attribute	Ethernet	IEEE 802.3	IEEE 802.5	ATM
Application support?	Asynchronous data (with some voice, but not designed for voice)	Asynchronous data (with some voice [but not designed for voice])	Asynchronous data	Asynchronous, synchronous voice, video, data
Connection mode?	Connectionless	Connectionless	Connectionless	Connection-oriented
Congestion management?	Collision detection	Collision detection	Priority (8 levels), and the passing of a token	Congestion notification, traffic tagging (CLP bit), and possibly traffic discard
Method of identifying traffic?	48-bit MAC address	48-bit MAC address	48-bit MAC address	Virtual circuit id: The VPI/VCI and an ATM address during connection setup
Congestion notification technique?	None	None	None	The CN bits in the PTI field
Traffic tagging technique?	None	None	None	The cell loss priority (CLP) bit
PDU size?	Variable	Variable	Variable	Fixed at 53 bytes (PDU is called a cell)
Sequencing of traffic?	No	No	No	Cell header, no; for payload, depends on payload type
Encapsulation header?	Yes, Ethertype	Yes, LLC header	Yes, LLC header	Typically LLC header
ACKs/NAKs/ retransmissions?	No	No	No	Only for signaling traffic (SVCs)

CLP	Cell loss priority	MAC	Media access control
CN	Congestion notification	PDU	Protocol data unit
DE	Discard eligibility	SVC	Switch virtual calls
LAN	Local area network	VCI	Virtual channel identifier
LLC	Logical link control	VPI	Virtual path identifier

Table 1–3   Comparisons of IP and ATM Technologies

Attribute	IP	ATM
Application support?	Asynchronous data (with some voice and video, but not so designed)	Asynchronous, synchronous voice, video, data
Connection mode?	Connectionless	Connection-oriented
Congestion management?	None	Congestion notification, traffic tagging (CLP bit), and possibly traffic discard
Method of identifying traffic?	32-bit IP address	Virtual circuit id: The VPI/VCI and an ATM address
Congestion notification technique?	None	The CN bits in the PTI field
Traffic tagging technique?	None	The cell loss priority (CLP) bit
PDU size?	Variable	Fixed at 53 bytes (PDU is called a cell)
Sequencing of traffic?	No	Cell header, no; for payload, depends on payload type
Encapsulation header?	Yes, IP Protocol ID (IP PID)	Typically LLC header
ACKs/NAKs/ retransmissions?	No	Only for signaling traffic (SVCs)

CONVENTIONS FOR ATM INTERFACES AND DATA UNITS

Figure 1–3 shows the conventions for the ATM and AAL layers, as well as the placement of service access points (SAPs) and the naming conventions. This information is discussed in more detail in Volume I of this series, but we revisit SAPs in Chapter 2.

Figure 1–3 is largely self-explanatory. It can be seen that the naming conventions follow the OSI conventions and use the concepts of service data units (SDUs), protocol data units (PDUs), primitives, encapsulation, decapsulation, and protocol control information (PCIs).

The AAL type 5 structure contains the convergence sublayer, which is divided into the common part convergence sublayer (CPCS) and the service specific convergence sublayer (SSCS) and is shown in Figure 1–4. The SSCS is used to support different user applications, and thus, multiple

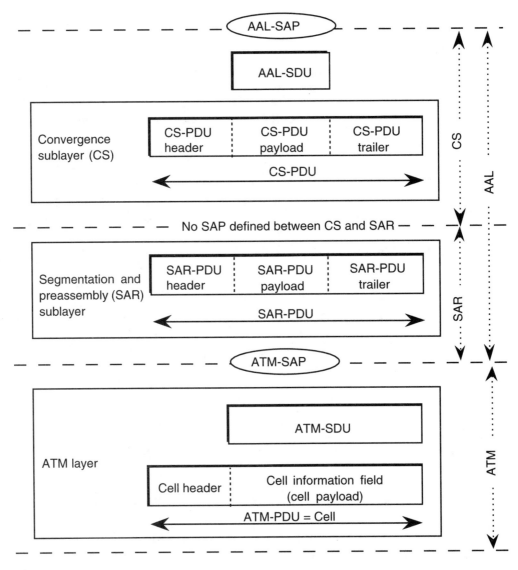

where:
PDU   Protocol data unit
SAP   Service access point
SDU   Service data unit

Figure 1–3   AAL general data unit conventions.

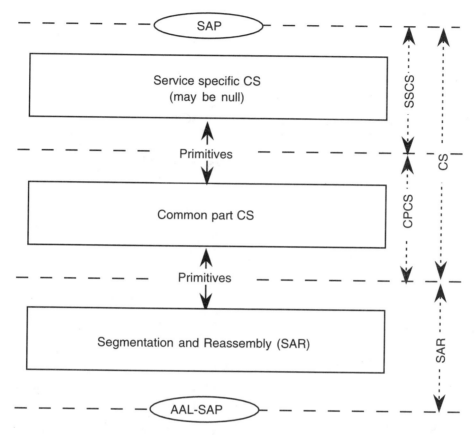

Figure 1–4   The AAL 5 structure.

SSCSs may exist. The SSCS may be null if it is not needed. In this case, it is used only to map primitives of the user upper layer to/from CPCS.

SUMMARY

Internetworking allows the users of different networks to exchange information with each other, and the deployment of ATM backbones to support other networks is consistent with the trend toward the increased use of ATM.

Carriers and service providers can accommodate the continuing growth of Frame Relay, LAN, and Internet services and integrate ATM features at the same time. ATM offers high-speed trunks that permit the negotiation of quality of service (QOS) features, such as delay, throughput, and peak burst rate features that most other technologies do not offer.

2

Encapsulation and Address Mapping Operations

This chapter describes the works of the standards bodies that have published a number of specifications defining (a) how traffic from different networks is transported through another network (for example, an ATM network), and (b) how the header in the PDUs of these different networks is (or is not) translated into the transporting network header.

This chapter also explains how MAC L_2 addresses, IP L_3 addresses, Frame Relay addresses, ATM addresses, and ATM/Frame Relay virtual circuit IDs are correlated with each other through address resolution protocols.

Some of the specifications that are examined in this chapter are generic, in that they do not define ATM per se. We will examine these specifications from the generic standpoint, as well as how they are used in ATM networks.

ENCAPSULATION CONCEPTS

The term encapsulation refers to an operation in which a transport (backbone) network, such as Ethernet, ATM, or Frame Relay, carries traffic (PDUs) from other protocols through the transport network. The other protocols could be IP, AppleTalk, SNA, DECnet, and so on that operate at the upper layers of the OSI layered model, typically at layer 3 and above. The transport network performs lower layer bearer services, typically at layers 1 and 2, and perhaps layer 3 of the model (but not always ... nothing is simple in internetworking ...).[1]

If possible, the transport network does not become involved with either the syntax or the format of the transported traffic. The term encapsulation refers to the notion of the interworking unit (say, a router) "wrapping" the *transport* PDU around the *user* SDU, without consideration to its contents.

Some people use the terms encapsulation and tunneling synonymously. Others use the term tunneling to describe the notion of sending traffic (say a car) through a "tunnel," and periodically stopping the car, rolling down the windows of the car and checking the contents in the passenger space. In other words, some definitions of tunneling suggest that the contents of the PDU may be examined during the transport operations. In this book, I will use the term encapsulation to describe both of these concepts.

To invoke encapsulation operations, the user must furnish the network with a specific identifier to distinguish the type of traffic that is to be sent through the transport network. This identifier is important, because the IWU and the receiving user machine must invoke support procedures that apply to the specific type of traffic; that is, a specific protocol family, such as X.25, IP, or SNA. After all, an IWU, such as a router, cannot process the PDU until it knows the type of PDU, such as its header contents and syntax.

These identifiers are depicted in Figure 2–1. They are known by various names, and vary in how they are used. They are examined in the next section of this chapter.

As we examine these encapsulation identifiers, keep in mind that some of them perform the same functions, and indeed are redundant. The reason that overlapping identifiers exist is that they have been developed by different standards groups and have evolved and changed over time.

Anyway, after each of these identifiers are examined, we will then learn about the overlaps of their functions, and how this overlap is handled in ATM encapsulations.

---

[1]Bearer services is a term used by most standards bodies to describe the basic telecommunications services that are available to the user of a network. They support services such as throughput (in bit/s) and delay (in ms).

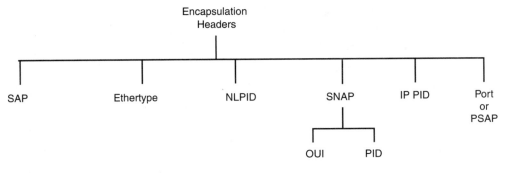

where:
    IP PID   IP Protocol ID
    NLPID   Network level protocol ID
    OUI   Organization unique ID
    PID   Protocol ID
    PSAP   Presentation layer SAP
    SAP   Service access point
    SNAP   Subnetwork access protocol

Figure 2–1   Options for encapsulation headers.

SERVICE ACCESS POINTS (SAPS)

In most systems, the services invoked at a layer are requested by the upper layers passing primitives (transactions) to the next lower layer. The primitives are usually coded into program function calls or system library calls and are used to identify the type of service needed, such as a connection or the transfer of traffic over the connection. Services are provided from the lower layer to the upper layer through a service access point (SAP). The SAP is an identifier. It identifies the entity or process in (say) layer $N - 1$ that is performing the service(s) for layer N (see Figure 2–2).

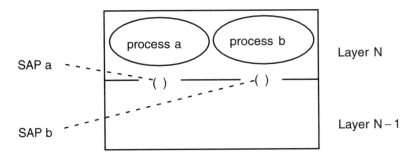

Figure 2–2   OSI service access points (SAPs).

An entity in machine A can invoke some services in machine B through the use of SAPs. For example, a user that sends traffic can identify itself with a source SAP id (SSAP). It identifies the recipient of the traffic with a destination SAP value (DSAP).

Some people view the SAP as a software "port." It is akin to the socket concept found in the UNIX operating system environment. In Figure 2–2, SAP a identifies a process (process a) in layer N, and SAP b identifies another process (process b). Examples of processes and their associated processes are (1) a signaling module, such as ATM's Q.2931, (2) a route discovery module, such as the Intermediate System-to-Intermediate System (IS-IS) protocol, and (3) the Connectionless Network Layer Protocol (CLNP).

LLC and LSAPs

The IEEE 802 LAN standards require the use of Link SAPs (LSAPs). As shown in Figure 2–3, an LSAP identifies the entity that resides above logical link control (LLC). Likewise, a MAC SAP (MSAP) identifies a particular LSAP entity operating above MAC, and a physical layer SAP (PLSAP) identifies a process operating above the physical layer (in the MAC layer).

In many installations, the PLSAPs and MSAPs are not employed. However, the LSAP is a common tool used by many vendors to provide interfaces into and out of LLC from the vendor network layer entities

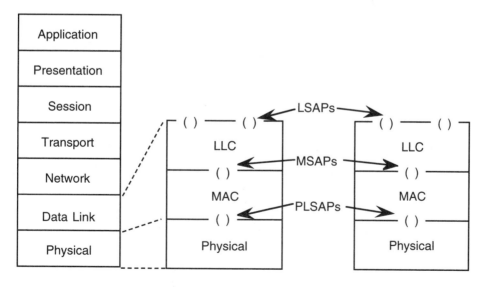

Figure 2–3　The SAPs.

such as IP, CLNP, and so on. In effect, the LSAP performs the same function as Ethertype, discussed next.

ETHERTYPE (TYPE)

The Ethertype (also called type or protocol type) field in an Ethernet frame is used to identify different protocols that are running on the Ethernet network (see Figure 2–4). Well-known protocols are registered and given a reserved value. As examples, IP is Ethertype = 0x0800, X.25 = 0x0805, ARP = 0x0806, RARP = 0x0835, AppleTalk = 0x8098, ect.

SUBNETWORK ACCESS PROTOCOL (SNAP)

Due to the separate evolution of the Ethernet, TCP/IP, and IEEE LAN standards, it has been necessary to define additional procedures to provide guidance on the use of IP datagrams over Ethernet and IEEE networks. Figure 2–5 shows the approach specified by RFC 1042 (A Standard for the Transmission of IP Datagrams over IEEE 802 Networks). RFC 1042 defines an extension to the LLC header, called the Subnetwork Access Protocol (SNAP).

The LLC destination and source service access points (DSAP and SSAP, respectively) are each set to a decimal value of 170 (0xAA). The LLC control field is not affected by this standard. This control field is

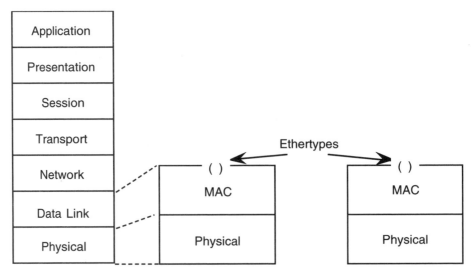

Figure 2–4   The Ethertype field.

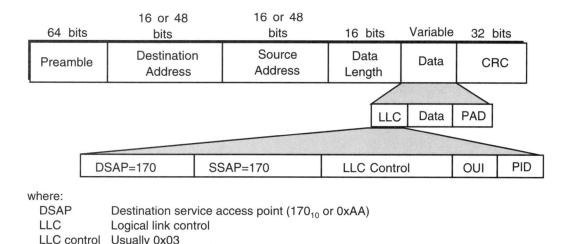

where:
DSAP   Destination service access point (170_{10} or 0xAA)
LLC   Logical link control
LLC control Usually 0x03
OUI   Organization unique ID
PID   SNAP protocol ID
SNAP   Subnetwork service access protocol
SSAP   Source service access point (170_{10} or 0xAA)

Figure 2–5   The Subnetwork Access Protocol (SNAP) format (RFC 1042).

based on the L_2 protocol, High Level Data Link Control (HDLC). In most LLC systems, this field is coded as 0x03 to identify an LLC type 1 PDU, which is an HDLC unnumbered information (UI) control field.

The SNAP control field identifies an organization unique ID (OUI) and a specific protocol ID (PID). Thereafter, the Ethertype field is often coded to describe the type of protocol running on the LAN. The Ethertype field is coded in accordance with the standard conventions. This figure shows the convention for coding the LSAP values (i.e., 170) for the SNAP convention.

The SNAP OUI and PID contents can vary, depending upon the technology using SNAP. For example, the original RFC 1042 sets OUI to 0 to indicate the PID is an ethertype value, but other implementations of SNAP use the field to identify how the field is employed, such as the enterprise or technology that is using the code for its own purposes. Many examples are provided in this book on the use of the SNAP OUI and PID.

ISO/IEC TR 9577 (NETWORK LEVEL PROTOCOL IDENTIFIER [NLPID])

The network level protocol identifier (NLPID) contains values to identify common protocols that are used in the industry, such as Connectionless Network Layer Protocol (CLNP), X.25, ect. It is administered by the International Standards Organization (ISO). The purpose of this field is to inform the receiver which protocol is being carried inside the transporting PDU frame.

The reader can obtain ISO/IEC TR 9577 for the values that are currently administered by the ISO. Examples of NLPIDs values are as follows. Note the provision for the use of the SNAP header (0x80), and IP(0xCC).

    0x00 Null network layer
    0x80 IEEE SNAP
    0x81 ISO CLNP
    0x82ISO ES-IS
    0x83 ISO IS-IS
    0xCC IP
    0x08ISDN Q.933

EXAMPLES OF JOINT USE OF NLPID AND SNAP

Some protocols do not have an assigned NLPID. In this situation, the subnetwork access protocol (SNAP) header can be used, and the NLPID is set to indicate that a SNAP header is present. Figure 2–6

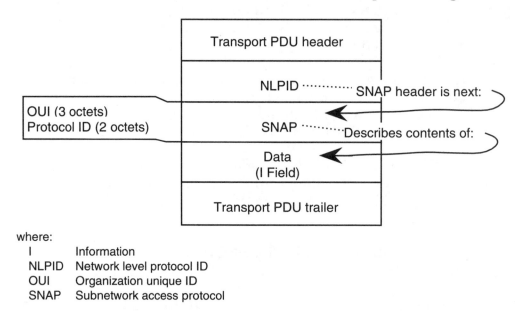

where:
    I   Information
    NLPID   Network level protocol ID
    OUI   Organization unique ID
    SNAP   Subnetwork access protocol

Figure 2–6   Use of the NLPID and SNAP headers.

shows the PDU for this approach. If the SNAP header is used, it is placed into the PDU immediately following the NLPID field.

IP PROTOCOL ID

The IP protocol field (IP PID) resides in the IP datagram header (a layer 3 header) and is used to identify the next protocol beyond IP that is to receive the IP datagram (see Figure 2–7). It is similar in function to the Ethertype field found in the Ethernet frame, but identifies the "next" entity beyond IP that is to receive and process the traffic, whereas Ethertype identifies an entity such as IP. The Internet standards groups have established a numbering system to identify widely used upper-layer protocols. As examples, TCP is 6 and UDP is 17.

The IP PID may also indicate the presence of another layer 3 header, in which case, the traffic is passed to it. For example, the Open Shortest Path First (OSPF) is a layer 3 protocol, and OSPF PDUs are transported through an internet with IP headers. At the receiving OSPF entity, the IP PID is used to pass the OSPF PDU to the OSPF module.

PORTS/PSAPS

Yet another encapsulation header is a port (an Internet term) or a presentation layer SAP (PSAP, an OSI term). This value is used to iden-

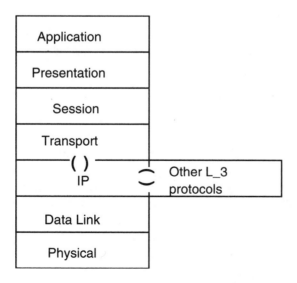

Figure 2–7 The IP protocol ID.

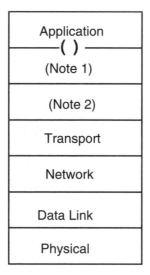

Note 1:   For OSI, the presentation layer. For Internet, TCP, or UDP.
Note 2:   For OSI, the session layer. For Internet, session layer not used.

Figure 2–8   The Port.

tify a process residing in the application layer (layer 7) of the conventional layered model.

The port operation is used more often than the PSAP, because it is part of the Internet protocol stack. Figure 2–8 shows that the layer under layer 7 uses the port number to identify the next (and last) process to receive the traffic.

The Internet reserves ports 1–1023 for common layer 7 protocols with "well-known ports". Some examples are: Telnet = 23, FTP = 20 and 21, and Domain Name System = 53.

PUTTING IT ALL TOGETHER

As stated earlier, some of these encapsulation headers perform the same functions. We will use Figure 2–9 to explain these redundancies and the overall relationships of the encapsulation headers. The figure illustrates the layered architecture for an internet system that operates with five layers of the conventional OSI Model. The layers are listed in the legend to the figure. User traffic is sent through the layers, as illustrated on the left side of the figure, from the sending side and is processed through the receiving protocol stack, which is illustrated on the right side of the figure.

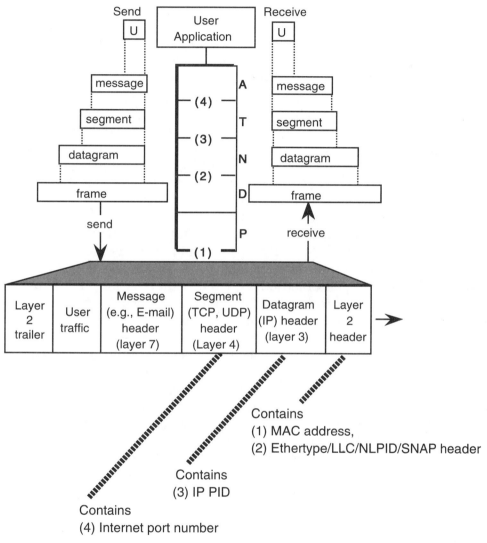

Figure 2–9   The encapsulation headers.

where:
- A Application layer
- T Transport layer
- N Network layer
- D Data link layer
- P Physical layer

The sending side performs conventional encapsulation functions by placing protocol control information (PCI) (headers and/or trailers) around the data unit that it is processing. At the receiving side, conventional decapsulation operations are performed with the PCI stripped away at the respective layer and processed by an identified entity in the layer. The bottom part of Figure 2–9 shows how the traffic is transported across the communications link in relation to the position of the headers and trailers.

The previous paragraph stated that an identified entity in a layer processes its respective header and that is the purpose of the encapsulation header: identify that entity. This idea is illustrated in Figure 2–9 with the use of the numbered notations (1), (2), (3), and (4). They are placed at the layer boundaries to symbolize where the interpretation of each encapsulation header is performed. Also notice that these numbers identify the specific encapsulation headers shown at the bottom of the figure. For the encapsulation header identified as (2), it should now be evident that there are several encapsulation headers performing the same or nearly the same function. But as I stated earlier, nothing is straightforward with this methodology. For example, an NLPID header could be coded to connote that a SNAP header follows in the PDU. Further, the SNAP header could indicate that an Ethertype field follows in the next field of the PDU. This rather confused approach is the result of the evolution of these methods through different standards groups with different agenda.

As we shall see as we proceed through this book, many of the internetworking operations must translate between the different encapsulation methods that are employed with a specific technology. For example, when internetworking ATM with Frame Relay the NLPID-based approach in Frame Relay must be mapped to the LLC-based approach in ATM.

Example of Encapsulation Operations

We proceed further to show how internetworking encapsulation operations are performed by using Figure 2–10 as an illustration. Remember that internetworking is performed for local area, wide area, and point-to-point or multipoint systems, as shown in Figure 2–10a. Regardless of the source or destination networks, the traffic passed to an IWU must contain an encapsulation header that identifies the type of traffic in the PDU (such as SNA, IP, X.25, etc.). This process is depicted in Figure 2–10b.

Figure 2–11 shows how the user traffic can be interpreted and transported through the ATM network. The boundary of the message

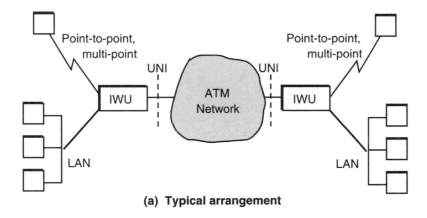

(a) Typical arrangement

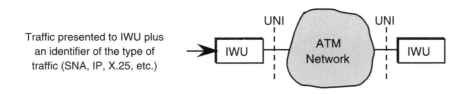

(b) Getting started

where:
IWU   Interworking unit

Figure 2–10   Using ATM as the transport network.

flow is between a calling user and a called user. In this example, the flow is between interworking units (IWU)—that is, routers.

The manner in which the end-user stations communicate with the routers is not defined by ATM, since the information flow between the end-user station and the router is not part of the ATM interface (at this time). Nonetheless, the user station-to-router operation is well defined in other standards, and the router need only map the information received from the user stations into the ATM AAL PDU at the originating router and perform a complementary and reverse operation at the terminating router.

Figure 2–11 also shows the operations for a LAN-to-LAN transmission with event-by-event notations, so I shall not elaborate further, but later discussions will focus in more detail on these operations.

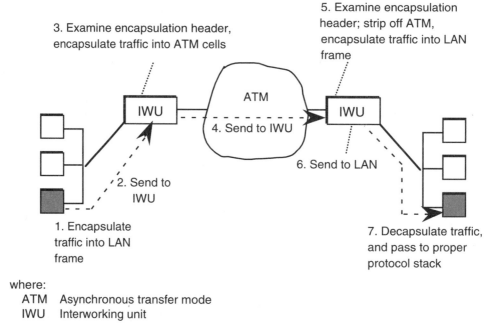

Figure 2–11   Example of an encapsulation procedure (a LAN-to-LAN example).

SUPPORT FOR LAYER 2 AND 3 PROTOCOLS

Figure 2–12 illustrates the various layer 2 and 3 protocols and procedures that can be identified in the encapsulation operations. Figure 2–12a depicts the layer 2 protocols, and Figure 2–12b depicts the layer 3 protocols.

For the layer 3 protocols, the LAN stations ordinarily support the Internet Protocol (IP), or some vendor-specific protocol, such as Novell Netware IPX. The approximate equivalent in this specification is ISO 8473, the connectionless network protocol, or CLNP.

Also, the subnetwork access protocol (SNAP) is employed in some systems to identify the layer 3 protocol that resides in the data unit. Nothing precludes using other methods. The most common approach is to use SNAP on LANs, as it was so designed, and to use the Point-to-Point (PPP) protocol on point-to-point links, as it was so designed.

LAPD, Q.922,LAPB, MLP,
ABM HDLC, ISO 7776,
X.75 SLP

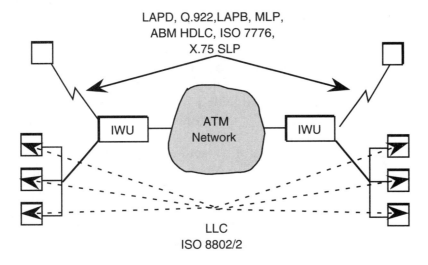

LLC
ISO 8802/2

(a) Layer 2 protocols

X.25, 8208,
8473, T.70, ISO

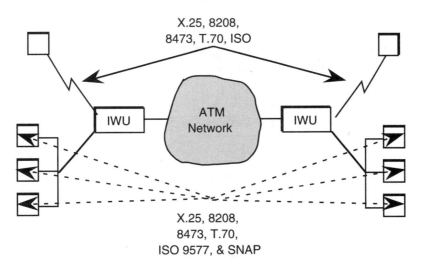

X.25, 8208,
8473, T.70,
ISO 9577, & SNAP

(b) Layer 3 protocols and SNAP

where:
ABM	Asynchronous balanced mode
HDLC	High level data link protocol
LAPD/B	Link access procedure, D channel/balanced
LLC	Logical link control
MLP	Multilink procedure
SLP	Single link procedure
SNAP	Subnetwork access protocol

Figure 2–12   Layers 2 and 3 identifications.

ENCAPSULATION RULES FOR FRAME RELAY (RFC 1490)

The Internet standard Request for Comments (RFC) 1490 establishes the rules for how protocols are encapsulated within the Frame Relay frame and transported across a network. This proposal is based on the encapsulation standards published in ANSI T1.617, Annex F. The Frame Relay Forum has used these documents as the basis for its Implementation Agreements (IAs).

This section provides a broad overview of RFC 1490. Be aware that RFC 1490 has many features and provides for various encapsulation operations. This section shows one option with the use of the NLPID. More options are described in Chapter 6.

As shown in Figure 2–13, traffic is carried in the Frame Relay frame, with the network level protocol identifier (NLPID) field used to identify which protocol family is contained in the I field of the frame. The

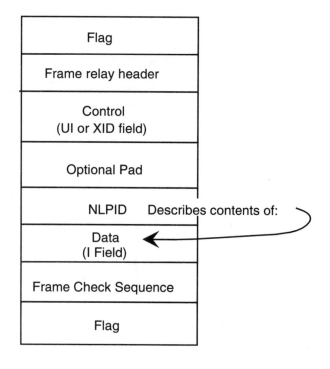

where:
   I   Information
  NLPID Network level protocol ID
  UI   Unnumbered information
  XID   Exchange ID

Figure 2–13   Encapsulation scheme for Frame Relay.

control field contains the HDLC unnumbered information (UI) field, or the XID field. The pad field is used to align the full frame to a 2-octet boundary.

For ongoing traffic, the UI control field is used. The XID control field can be employed during an initialization operation between the user stations to negotiate (1) maximum frame size, (2) the retransmission timer, and (3) the window size (maximum number of permitted outstanding I frames allowed).

We leave RFC 1490 for the time being. More detailed examples of Frame Relay encapsulation are provided in Chapter 6 (see "Bridged PDUs", "Routed IP PDUs", and "Routed OSI PDUS" sections).

ENCAPSULATION RULES FOR ATM (RFC 1483)

The Internet standard Request for Comments (RFC) 1483 establishes the rules for how protocols are encapsulated within the AAL 5 PDU and transported across a network. RFC 1483 supports a number of options and is similar to its Frame Relay counterpart, RFC 1490, just discussed. It uses the conventional AAL 5 PDU format that is described in Volume I of this series, with some special rules that are summarized here.

In the same manner that we examined RFC 1490, this section provides a broad overview of RFC 1483, which has many features and provides for various encapsulation operations. This section shows one option with the use of AAL 5. Once again, Chapter 6 depicts some more options. Also, Chapter 3 has other information on RFC 1483 (See "Guidance from RFC 1483").

Figure 2–14 shows the format of the type 5 PDU. It consists of an 8-octet trailer. The PAD field acts as a filler to fill out the CPCS-PDU to

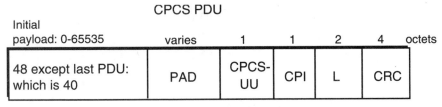

where:
  CPCS-UU   Common part convergence sublayer-user to user indication
  CPI   Common part indicator
  CRC   Cyclic redundancy check
  L   Length
  Payload   CPCS-PDUs

Figure 2–14   The AAL type 5 PDU.

48 octets. The CPCS-UU field not processed, since it has no function under RFC 1483. The common part indicator (CPI) has not been fully defined in ITU-T I.363. The length field (L) defines the payload length, and the CRC field is used to detect errors in the SSCS PDU (user data).

Type 5 is a convenient service for Frame Relay because it supports connection-oriented services. In essence, the Frame Relay user traffic is given to an ATM backbone network for transport to another Frame Relay user.

Options in RFC 1483

RFC defines two methods of sending connectionless traffic over ATM (this traffic can be bridged PDUs (L_2) or routed PDUs (L_3)). The first method supports multiplexing multiple protocols over a single ATM virtual circuit. Using this method, the PDU protocol is identified by an LLC header. The second method requires that the transported protocol be identified by the ATM VC.

The values and meanings for the LLC encapsulation method are shown in Table 2–1. The PID for bridged PDUs can have more than one value. One value indicates that the FCS (frame check sequence) in the PDU is to be preserved. The other value indicates that the FCS is not preserved.

We leave RFC 1483 for a while, but revisit it in the chapters/sections cited earlier, and show several detailed examples in Chapter 6. (See "Bridged PDUs", "Routed IP PDUs", and "Routed OSI PDUs" sections).

Table 2–1   LLC Values

LLC Value	Meaning
0xFE-FE-03	Routed ISO PDUs (1)
0xAA-AA-03	Presence of SNAP header (2)
0xAA-AA-03	Presence of SNAP header (3)

(1) Routed ISO protocol is identified by NLPID that is part of the PDU

(2) OUI of 0x00-00-00 indicates that the following SNAP PID is an Ethertype valve

(3) OUI of 0x00-80-02 identifies the IEEE 802.1 organization code followed by PID which identifies the type of bridged media: (a) 802.3 (b) 802.4, (c) 802.5, (d) FDDI, (e) 802.6 and (f) a bridge PDU

THE ADDRESS RESOLUTION PROTOCOL (ARP)

The Internet publishes a protocol for resolving addresses. Resolving addresses means the association (correlation) of one address to another. The Address Resolution Protocol (ARP) is used to take care of the translation of L_3 addresses to physical addresses (also known as hardware addresses, link addresses, and L_2 addresses) and hide these addresses from the upper layers.

The operation of ARP is important because most networks use more than one address. In the TCP/IP suite, for example, the IP L_3 address is used to route traffic through a wide area internet (and must be available for TCP/IP to function correctly), whereas a MAC L_2 address is used to reach a host attached to a LAN. Both addresses are required for the two systems to communicate with each other.

Generally, ARP works with mapping tables (referred to as ARP cache). For example, the table provides the mapping between an IP address and a physical address. The term physical address is used in ARP to describe a lower layer address. This book uses the terms, MAC and L_2 address for physical address. In a LAN (like Ethernet or an IEEE 802 network), ARP takes a target IP address and searches for a corresponding "target" physical address (a 48-bit MAC address) in a mapping table. If it finds the address, it returns the 48-bit MAC address back to the requester, such as a work station or server on a LAN. However, if the needed address is not found in the ARP cache, the ARP module sends a broadcast onto the network (assuming the network is a LAN).

The broadcast is called the ARP request. The ARP request contains a target IP address. Consequently, if one of the machines receiving the broadcast recognizes its IP address in the ARP request, it will return an ARP reply back to the inquiring host. This message contains the hardware address of the queried host and its IP address. Upon receiving this datagram, the ARP requestor places this address mapping into the ARP cache. Thereafter, datagrams sent to this particular IP address can be translated to the physical address.

The ARP protocol thus allows an inquiring node to find the physical address of another node by using the IP address.

The concepts of ARP requests and replies are shown in Figure 2–15. Host A wishes to determine C's physical address (say, an Ethernet address). It broadcasts to B, C, and D. Only C responds because it recognizes its IP address in the incoming ARP request message. Host C places its IP and MAC addresses in the ARP reply. The other hosts, B and D, do not respond.

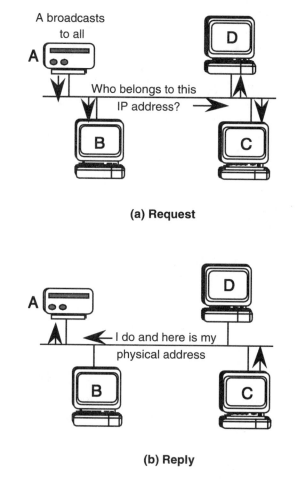

(a) Request

(b) Reply

Figure 2–15   The Address Resolution Protocol (ARP) request and reply.

In addition to the mapping of IP addresses to physical addresses, ARP also allows the designation of specific hardware types. Therefore, when an ARP message is received by the queried host, it can use a field in the datagram to determine if the machine is using a particular type of hardware such as an Ethernet interface, packet radio, and so on.

The operations shown in Figure 2–15 can be invoked at a host by issuing a function called gethostbyname. This routine uses a name server operation (the Domain Name System [DNS]) to map a name to a L_3 address (an IP address).

The entries in the ARP cache are managed with a timer. Most systems will time-out the entry after 20 minutes, although entries can be entered by the system administrator that do not time-out.

The ARP Protocol Data Units (PDUs)

The format for the ARP message is shown in Figure 2–16. The first part of the message is the header of the Ethernet frame, consisting of the MAC addresses and the Ethertype field. Thereafter, the hardware type and protocol type describe the types of addresses that are to be "resolved." The term hardware refers to a physical, link layer address, and the term protocol refers to an upper layer address, typically a L_3 address, such as IP, X.25, or IPX .

The length fields explain how long the address fields are, and for Ethernet and IP addresses, they are 6 and 4 octets respectively. The sending address fields identify the addresses of the sending entity. The target addresses are those that need resolving. In a typical ARP request, the target hardware address is left blank, and in the reply, it is filled in by the responding station.

Octets

Destination Address	6
Source Address	6
Ethertype	2
Hardware type	2
Protocol type	2
Hardware length	1
Protocol length	1
Op code	2
Sending hardware address	6
Sending protocol address	4
Target hardware address	6
Target protocol address	4

Figure 2–16   The ARP PDU.

FRAME RELAY ARP

Address resolution in a Frame Relay network works in a similar manner as I just described in a conventional environment. Figure 2–17 shows how ARP is used with Frame Relay. Be aware that the approach described here does not use ARP in its conventional manner. The hardware address fields in the ARP messages are used to contain Frame Relay DLCIs, and pure, modular OSI layering concepts are not used. Also, the ARP hardware type is 15 (0x00-0F), which is assigned to Frame Relay.

Keep in mind for this operation that Frame Relay DLCIs have local significance, and a user device (such as a router) uses a DLCI based on an agreement with the network.

To begin the process, user A forms an ARP request message. Since hardware addresses are not used initially in this process, the hardware address fields are undefined in the ARP request message. The source and destination protocol addresses (for example, IP addresses) are filled in as usual. In this example, the source IP address is A (for user A) and the destination IP address is D (for user D).

User A encapsulates its L_3 traffic into a frame and places DLCI 15 in the frame header. This value was assigned previously (usually by the network). The object is to associate DLCI 15 and IP address D with a remote DLCI. When user D receives the ARP request, it is encapsulated into the frame header, which contains the local DLCI value of 56 (placed into the frame by the Frame Relay network). User D extracts this value from the header and places it in the source hardware address of the incoming ARP request message. This process allows user D to associate protocol address A (in the source protocol address field) with DLCI 56. The box on the right side of the figure shows where the correlation takes place.

Next, user D forms the ARP response message (exchanges the source and destination values in the message), but leaves the destination hardware address undefined (which of course becomes defined when the source and destination addresses are exchanged). When user A receives this frame, it has DLCI 15 in the Frame Relay header. Thus, user A extracts this value and places it in the source hardware address field of the message. This operation allows user A to correlate DLCI 15 to protocol address D. Once again, the two boxes in this figure highlight where the correlations take place.

After these operations have taken place, users A and B know the following facts:

- User A knows that address D is correlated with its local DLCI 15
- User D knows that address A is correlated with its local DLCI 56

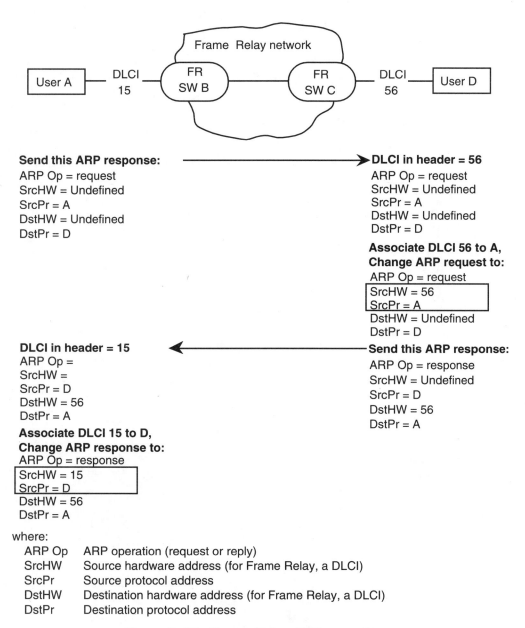

Send this ARP response:
ARP Op = request
SrcHW = Undefined
SrcPr = A
DstHW = Undefined
DstPr = D

DLCI in header = 56
ARP Op = request
SrcHW = Undefined
SrcPr = A
DstHW = Undefined
DstPr = D

Associate DLCI 56 to A,
Change ARP request to:
ARP Op = request
SrcHW = 56
SrcPr = A
DstHW = Undefined
DstPr = D

DLCI in header = 15
ARP Op =
SrcHW =
SrcPr = D
DstHW = 56
DstPr = A

Associate DLCI 15 to D,
Change ARP response to:
ARP Op = response
SrcHW = 15
SrcPr = D
DstHW = 56
DstPr = A

Send this ARP response:
ARP Op = response
SrcHW = Undefined
SrcPr = D
DstHW = 56
DstPr = A

where:

ARP Op	ARP operation (request or reply)
SrcHW	Source hardware address (for Frame Relay, a DLCI)
SrcPr	Source protocol address
DstHW	Destination hardware address (for Frame Relay, a DLCI)
DstPr	Destination protocol address

Figure 2–17   Frame Relay ARP operations.

CLASSICAL IP AND ARP OVER ATM (RFC 1577)

RFC 1577 defines the operations for encapsulating IP datagrams and ATM address resolution protocol (ATMARP) traffic over ATM and AAL5. Its principal concern is to specify the operation of IP over an ATM network and the resolving of IP addressees and ATM addresses. The idea is to allow ATM to replace (1) a LAN backbone, such as FDDI; (2) dedicated links between routers; (3) LANs (such as Ethernet, Token Ring, etc.); or (4) Frame Relay networks. The environment is established as a logical IP subnetwork (LIS).

RFC 1577 views ATM acting as a layer 2 transport service, which simply uses the IP over Ethernet idea and extends the concepts to ATM (IP over ATM).

IP subnetworks become LISs, which are internetworked by routers, as shown in Figure 2–18.

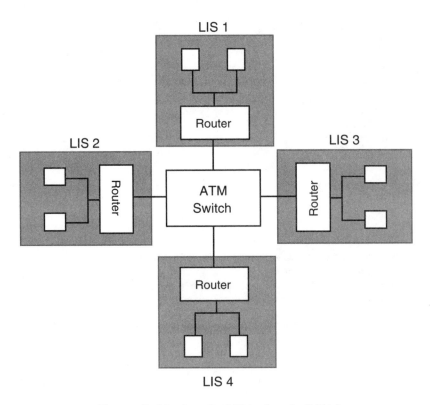

Figure 2–18   Logical IP subnets (LISs).

THE LIS CONFIGURATION

The LIS is configured with hosts and routers within a logical IP subnetwork. Each LIS communicates with each other through the same ATM network, although each LIS is independent of each other. Communication occurs through an IP router, which is configured as an ATM end point connected both to the ATM network and to one or more LISs. As a result of this configuration, multiple LISs might operate over the same ATM network. However, RFC 1577 requires that hosts operating on different LISs must communicate with each other through an intermediate router, even if they are attached to the same ATM network. This rule exists even though it is possible to establish a direct virtual channel between the two IP members over the ATM network. This rule is based on previous Internet standards dealing with IP host requirements, and relies on conventional protocols to interwork LISs. See RFC 1122.

Given this basic scenario, the operations are established with the following rules:

1. All IP members (which consist of hosts and routers) are directly connected to the ATM network.
2. All members must use the same IP network/subnetwork number as well as address mask.
3. Any member that is outside the LIS must be accessed via a router.
4. All members must be able to resolve IP addresses to ATM addresses through ATMARP.
5. All LIS members must be able to communicate via ATM with other members within the same LIS (this means that within a list membership connection topologies are fully meshed).
6. Address resolution must be performed for both PVCs and SVCs.

Each IP station connected to the ATM network must be configured with an ATM address (which is the ATM address of the individual station) as well as an ATMARP request address. This value is the ATM address of an ATMARP server located at the LIS. The idea is to permit this server to resolve IP and ATM addresses. The server must be able to resolve all ATMARP requests for all IP members in the LIS.

In addition, all operations must support the IEEE 802.2 LLC/SNAP encapsulation operations defined in RFC 1483.

A default maximum transmission unit size (MTU) for IP members is 9180 octets. Since the LLC/SNAP header consists of 8 octets, the default

AAL5 PDU is 9188 octets. Values other than the default can be used if all members of the LIS have be so configured.

RULES FOR ADDRESS RESOLUTION

The address resolution operations make use of the ATM address resolution protocol (ATMARP) and the inverse address resolution protocol (InATMARP). These specifications are published in RFC 826 and RFC 1293, respectively. The ATMARP is an extension of the original ARP protocol. Inverse ATMARP is the same protocol as the original inverse ARP published in RFC 1293 but altered for ATM operations.[2] The system also uses ATMARP servers, and clients, as shown in Figure 2–19.

InARP operates like ARP except InARP does not use broadcasting, since the hardware address of the destination station is already known. Therefore, for the InARP (and the ATM extension, InATMARP) operation, the requesting station constructs a request by placing its source ATM address, its source protocol address, and the known target destination ATM (AKA hardware) address in these fields. The responding station fills in the destination protocol address in the reply and uses the source addresses in the request as the target addresses for the reply. This completes the resolution of the L_3 and ATM addresses.

As stated earlier, the classical IP operations must support both PVCs and SVCs. For operations with PVCs, the IP members must use inverse ATMARP for the PVCs with LLC/SNAP, SNAP encapsulation. If the ATM source and/or target address is not known, the corresponding address length in the inverse ATM packet is set to zero, which indicates a no length. Otherwise, the address is filled into the field.

For switched virtual connections (SVCs), classical IP requires that an ATMARP server must be located within the LIS and it must have the responsibility for resolving any ATMARP requests with all members of the LIS. It is not the responsibility of the server to establish connections, but will depend on the clients within the LIS to initiate the ATMARP registration operations when a client connects to the ATMARP server with a point-to-point VC. Upon the completion of an ATM connection, the server will transmit an inverse ATMARP request to determine the IP address of the client. The client then will reply in the ATMARP reply message the information that the ATMARP server will need to build its

---

[2]RFC 1293 was published to resolve Frame Relay and L_3 addresses, but it applies to ATM, as well.

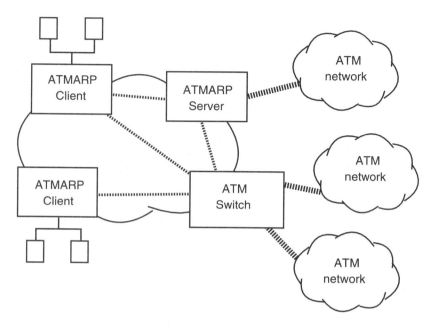

Figure 2–19   ATMARP clients and servers.

ATMARP table cache. Afterwards, this information is used to generate replies to the ATMARP queries that the server receives. Only one ATMARP server is allowed to operate per logical IP subnet, and the ATMARP server should also be an IP station. In addition, the ATMARP server must be configured with an IP address for each logical IP subnet that it serves in order to support all the inverse ATMARP requests.

Figure 2–20 shows these ideas in more detail (examples use IP class B addresses). An ATM backbone connects three subnetworks: 176.16.2, 176.16.3, and 176.16.4. Routers act as the interworking units between the legacy (conventional) LANs and the ATM backbone. The routers are also configured as LIS clients and access the LIS ARP server to obtain mappings between IP and ATM addresses.

Figure 2–21 provides another level of detail to Figure 2–20. Each node in the ATM network is configured with an ATM address and an IP address as follows:

	ATM Address	**IP Address**
LIS server	HIJ	172.16.1.1
LIS router/client	DEF	172.16.1.4
LIS router/client	ABC	172.16.1.3
LIS router/client	KLM	172.16.1.2

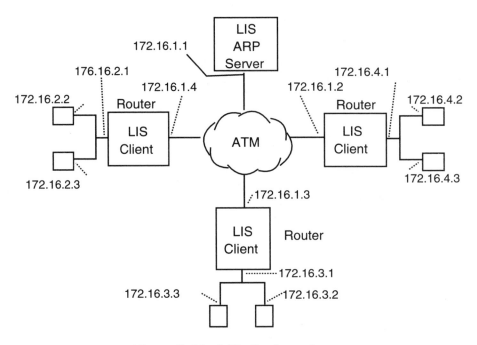

Figure 2–20   LIS clients and servers.

Figure 2–21 shows examples of entries in the routing table and ARP table stored at router KLM/172.16.1.2. The routing table contains the next node that is to receive the datagram based on the destination IP address in the IP datagram. The ARP table (cache) contains the IP and ATM address mappings (resolutions).

The creation of the routing table is through conventional route discovery protocols, such as OSPF. The creation of the ARP table is through ATMARP.

OPERATIONS AT THE ATMARP SERVER AND CLIENT

Operations at the Server

As mentioned earlier, the ATMARP server communicates with other ATM endpoints over ATM VCs shown in Figure 2–22. At the call setup operation, the ATMARP server will transmit to each originating ATM station the inverse ARP request message (InATMARP). A request is sent for each logical IP subnet that the server is configured to serve (bear in mind, configuration is required beforehand). The server then receives the InATMARP reply and examines the IP address and the correlated ATM

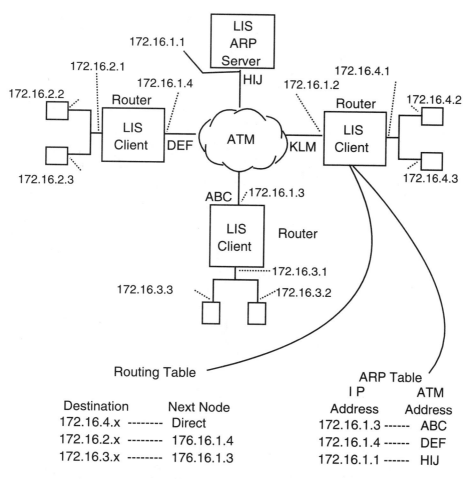

Figure 2–21   Routing table and ARP table (partial tables).

address. Based on this examination, the server then adds or deletes the ATM address, IP address entry into its ATMARP table. It also adds a timestamp to this entry at this time.

Thereafter, as mentioned earlier, the ATMARP server is responsible for receiving ATMARP requests and generating an appropriate ATMARP reply, if it has a proper entry in its ATMARP table. If it does not have an entry in this table, it will generate a negative ATMARP reply to the client.

Operations at the ATMARP Client Site

The ATMARP client must contact the ATMARP server to register its own information and to refresh any information that it has sent earlier.

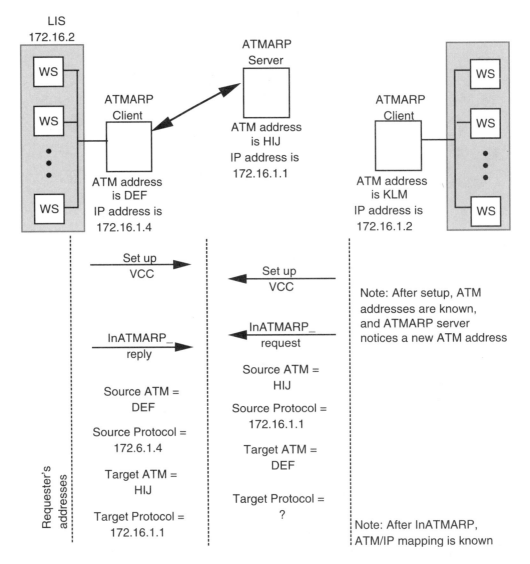

Figure 2–22   The InATMARP operations.

Consequently, the ATMARP client must be configured beforehand with the address of the ATMARP server. Once these configuration operations are put in place, the ATMARP client is responsible for the following:

- As just stated, it must initiate the VC connection to the ARP server.
- It must respond to ARP request and inverse ARP request packets.

- It must generate and transmit ARP request packets to the server and process ARP reply and ARP NAK packets from the server.
- The ARP reply packets must be used to refresh its own table entry.
- It must generate and transmit inverse ARP request packets as needed and to process inverse ARP reply packets as needed.
- It must provide an ATMARP table with an appropriate agent function in order to remove old entries after a period of time.

Figure 2–23 provides one final example of ATMARP (not InAT-MARP) operations. We assume that router A (also an ATMARP client)

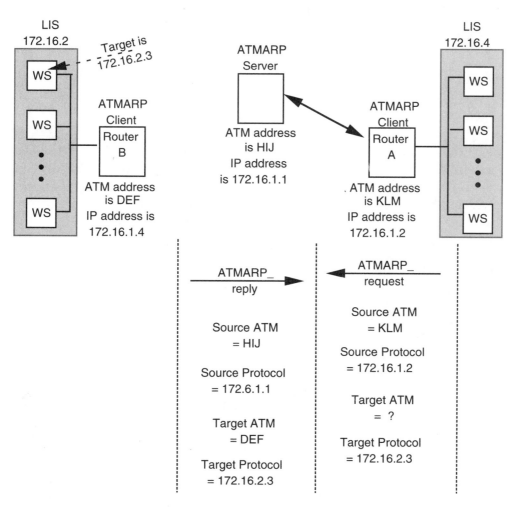

Figure 2–23   The ATMARP operations.

identified as KLM/172.16.1.2 receives a datagram from one of its work-stations (WS) with an IP destination address of 172.16.2.3. This data-gram should be forwarded across the ATM network to router B (DEF/172.16.1.4) for delivery to the destination workstation. If router A has the entry IP = 172.16.2—ATM = DEF in ARP cache, it knows the path to the destination. If it has no such entry, it constructs an ATMARP request message as shown in Figure 2–23 and sends the message to the ATMARP server. Because router B had previously registered its address with the server, this server can send back the ATMARP reply to router A, which now knows the path to the destination.

Notice that the ATMARP operation in Figure 2–23 is the opposite of the InATMARP operation in Figure 2–22:

InATMARP request: Target Protocol address is sought
ATMARP request: Target ATM address is sought

ATMARP AND INVERSE ATMARP PACKET FORMATS

Table 2–2 shows the formats for the ATMARP and inverse ATMARP packets. The formats are quite similar to the conventional ARP and inverse ARP protocols referenced earlier. Indeed, the hardware type, proto-col type, and operation code are the same between the two sets of proto-cols, and the location of these fields within the ATMARP packet are in the same position as in the ARP and inverse ARP packets. For ATMARP, a unique hardware type has been assigned and also ATMARP uses an additional operation code for ARP NAK.

ATMARP AND INATMARP PACKET ENCAPSULATION

The ATMARP and inverse ATMARP packets must be encoded in AAL5 PDUs using LLC/SNAP encapsulation. Figure 2–24 shows the for-mat for these encapsulations. The LLC of 0xAA-AA-03 indicates the pres-ence of a SNAP header. The OUI of 0x00-00-00 indicates the next two bytes are the Ethertype field, and the Ethertype field is coded as 0x08-06 to indicate ATMARP or InATMARP packets.

As stated earlier, the restriction of this simple classical model is due to its adherence to RFC 1122 ("Requirement for Internet hosts—Commu-nication Layers"): any datagram with a destination address other than the originator's subnet must go through a *default* router, even if a better

Table 2–2 Formats for ATMARP Packets

Name	Function	Size
Hardware type	Assigned to ATM Forum (0x00-13)	2
Protocol type	Based on Assigned numbers for protocol type using ATM. For example, IP is 0x08-00	2
Source ATM address/type length	Type and length of source ATM number (q)	1
Source ATM subaddress type/length	Type and length of source ATM subaddress (r)	1
Operation code	Operation code for packet (see Table 2–3)	2
Source protocol address length	Length of source protocol address (s)	1
Target ATM address/type length	Type and length of target ATM number (x)	1
Target ATM subaddress type/length	Type and length of target ATM subaddress (y)	1
Target protocol address length	Length of target protocol address (s)	1
Source ATM address	ATM source address	q
Source ATM subaddress	ATM source subaddress	r
Source protocol address	Protocol source address	s
Target ATM address	ATM target address	x
Target ATM subaddress	ATM target subaddress	y
Target protocol address	Protocol target address	z

path exists, say through an ATM backbone to hosts on multiple LISs. Also, the datagram must pass through the *intermediate* routers of any other LISs.

These deficiencies are addressed with other internetworking specifications, notably the next Hop Resolution Protocol, discussed in Chapter 10.

Table 2–3 Coding for the Operation Type

OP Code	Value
ARP_REQUEST	1
ARP_REPLY	2
InARP_REQUEST	8
InARP_REPLY	9
ARP_NAK	10

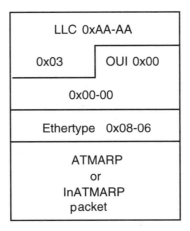

Figure 2–24   Encapsulation into AAL5 PDUs.

MULTICAST ADDRESS RESOLUTION SERVER (MARS)

Until recently, the ATM internetworking operations have focused on unicast operations. But for ATM to be an effective transport network it must support multicasting since LANs use multicasting extensively. Furthermore, IP multicasting is common today, especially with the use of Mbone (multicasting backbone), the Internet multicasting protocol.

To fix this problem (at least partially) the Multicast Address Resolution Server (MARS) specification is being developed. As of this writing, all issues surrounding MARS had not been resolved, but its definition is stable enough to warrant a discussion of its operations.

MARS is an extension to ARP and ATMARP. It maps L_3 multicast addresses to one or more ATM addresses. The mapping record is called a host map and contains the IP multicast address to/from the ATM addresses.

The MARS configuration is shown in Figure 2–25. The multicast server and client communicate initially through a bi-directional point-to-point (pt-pt) ATM VC, which is setup at the initiative of the client. The VC is used to transmit multicast resolution queries to the server. Each server manages a cluster of ATM end-points (clients), which represent a set of ATM interfaces.

Two types of VCs are defined for MARS operations. The first is the Cluster Control VC and is used to connect MARS to all end systems (cluster members). This link is a point-to-multipoint (pt-mpt) VC, and all

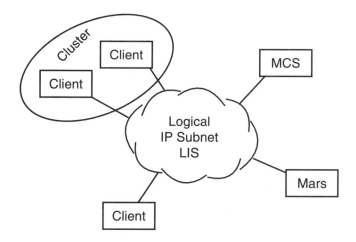

where
  MARS: Multicast Address Resolution Protocol Server
  MCS: Multicast Server

Figure 2–25   The MARS configuration.

members are leaf nodes. The second VC is the Server Control VC, which links MARS to all multicast servers (MCSs)—if MCSs are used. MARS does not define the role of the MCS. For more information on multicasting servers, see M. Macedonia and D. Brutzman. mBone, The Multicast Backbone, http://www.cs.ucl.ac.uk/mice/mbone_review.html

Before a datagram is sent by a client, it is determined if a multicast outbound path currently exists for the multicast address. If no path exists, the MARS is queried in a MARS_REQUEST message by the client for the appropriate ATM addresses for the operation. The paths could be to MCSs or the actual members of the multicast group. The MARS responds to the request message in one of two ways:

- Sends a MARS_NAK message: MARS has no mapping for the multicast address
- Sends a MARS_MULTI message: A match is found and the host map is sent to the client

Thereafter, a pt-mpt VC is created and the ATM endpoints in the host map are added to a multicast group.

Nodes can join and leave multicasting groups with the MARS_JOIN and MARS_LEAVE messages, that are sent via the Cluster Control VC. MCSs can also join and leave the system by using these messages.

Pros and Cons of MARS

MARS is a simple and effective approach for small environments with few nodes. It handles registration, queries, and "de-registration" in an efficient manner. However, several studies conclude that MARS will not scale well to larger systems, since multicast traffic must transit to a single multicast server. The problem also stems from the likely expanding of hosts and/or MCSs that must be connected with pt-mpt SVCs. IP multicast routing can reduce the magnitude of the problem, but the provisioning and management of the MARS mapping information still translates into considerable overhead.[3]

Notwithstanding, MARS is another useful tool and one more supplementary instrument in the ATM internetworking tool box.

SUMMARY

We learned in this chapter that encapsulation operations are used to identify the types of traffic that are carried in a protocol data unit. We have also learned that the concept of encapsulation is quite simple but overlapping encapsulation conventions and standards complicate the process.

The chapter also introduced address resolution with the focus on the Address Resolution Protocol (ARP) and its variations. This protocol is essential in internetworking operations because of its ability to resolve (correlate/map) from one address to another.

---

[3]For more information on this subject see G. Armitage, "VENUS—Very Extensive Non-Unicast Service", Internet Draft, 1997.

3

ATM/Frame Relay
Interworking Operations

This chapter introduces the basic operations for ATM/Frame Relay interworking. It sets the stage for more detailed discussions in subsequent chapters. Several interworking models are explained and a comparison is made between protocol encapsulation/protocol mapping and network interworking/service interworking.

The chapter also explains the use of the Frame Relay core service access point (CSAP), which provides guidance on building an application programming interface (API) on top of the Frame Relay layers. This chapter concludes by revisiting RFC 1483 (which was introduced in Chapter 2) in more detail.

ATM/FRAME RELAY INTERWORKING MODELS

The FR/ATM interworking function (IWF) can be implemented in two configurations:

- As a interworking service application, in which frame-to-cell adaptation is done at the edge of the subnet
- As a gateway between the frame and ATM subnetworks within a network

Using these two basic configurations, FR-ATM interworking can be deployed with three different models. Most implementations reflect this model, which is derived from Nortel's Magellan ATM Family.

1. *Frame Relay network leveraging another carrier's ATM network.* The frame-to-cell adaptation is done on the edge of the Frame Relay network, between the Frame Relay network and the carrier ATM network. This application is a FR-ATM gateway (see Figure 3–1a).

2. *Interconnected Frame Relay and ATM networks.* The frame-to-cell adaptation is done in the middle of the mixed network configuration, outside of the subnetworks. This application is also a gateway (see Figure 3–1b).

3. *ATM centric network.* The frame-to-cell adaptation is performed at the edge of the ATM network. This application uses the IWF in a FR-ATM interworking service implementation (see Figure 3–1c).

The FR-ATM IWF can be deployed within a single network in any combination and number of these models. Since networks are not static, most network topologies evolve from one model to another, or evolve to incorporate additional models, as traffic volumes, services, and tariffs evolve.

INTERNETWORKING DEFINITIONS

Protocol Encapsulation and Protocol Mapping

Before we begin an analysis of the internetworking relationships of Frame Relay and ATM, several definitions are in order. These definitions are extracted from ITU-T Recommendation I.555. First, *protocol encapsulation* describes an interworking function in which the conversions in the network or terminals are such that the protocols used to provide one service make use of the layer service provided by another protocol. This means that at the interworking point, the two protocols are stacked. In effect, this means that a protocol is encapsulated by either the network or the terminal.

In contrast, *protocol mapping* actually performs conversion. By this I mean that the protocol information of one protocol is extracted and mapped onto the protocol information of another protocol. This also means that each terminal can support different protocols and a common layer service is provided by the functions that are common to the two protocols.

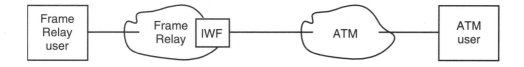

(a) Adaptation at edge of Frame Relay network

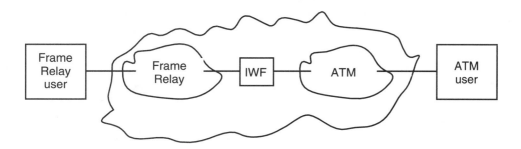

(b) Adaptation at middle of a mixed network

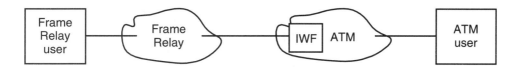

(c) Adaptation at edge of ATM network.

Figure 3–1   Deployment model.

Network and Service Interworking

Two other definitions that are used in this book are network interworking and service interworking.

Network interworking is an operation in which an ATM network connects two Frame Relay users *through* the ATM backbone.

Service interworking is similar to network interworking, but the ATM backbone connects a Frame Relay user to an ATM user.

GUIDES FOR THE USER INTERFACE

The ITU-T has published Annex C to I.233, which defines the relationship of the relaying bearer service to the OSI network layer service. This bearer service is intended to support the network layer service, in accordance with ITU-T Recommendation X.213. The value of this specification is that it defines the interface between a user application and the Frame Relay layer. Thus, it aids the programmer who is writing the application's programming interface (API) between a user application and Frame Relay.

OSI network service consists of three phases: (1) connection establishment, (2) data transfer, and (3) connection release. The connection establishment and release services are provided by Q.930 series, and the data transfer phase is provided by the Q.922 series, which is the ITU-T Frame Relay standards.

ITU-T requires that several functions be supported above Q.922: (1) segmentation/reassembly, (2) RESET, (3) a protocol discriminator, (4) expedited data, and (5) qualified data indication.

The actual transfer phase must be provided by a protocol that resides in the user end systems. This protocol must reside above the data link layer. That is to say, it must reside above Q.922. This end user protocol could be an existing X.25 protocol, a user specific protocol, or a connectionless protocol (such as ISO 8473, the connectionless network protocol [CLNP]).

The core service is made available through the core service access point (CSAP). The core service provides connection-oriented transparent transfer of data between core users. The core service must provide independence from any type of underlying physical layer. It is the function of core service to keep the user transparent from the physical layer with the exception of certain QOS features that depend on the physical layer (such as basic or primary data rates).

As depicted in Figure 3–2, the core service must also provide transparency of information transfer. This means that the user need not be concerned with the core layer interpreting the content of its data. Conversely, the core layer does not care about the content, syntax, coding, or format of the data it receives. Its only concern in this regard is that of the length of the core service data unit.

Primitive Operations

The core service must provide several features to the user above it. It must support connections that remain transparent to the end user (see Figure 3–3). Additionally, it must support certain QOS parameters that have been coordinated by the user through the use of the C-plane and perhaps the systems management plane.

It must provide a transparent connection and transfer of CSDUs on behalf of the user through the network. It must also be able to measure

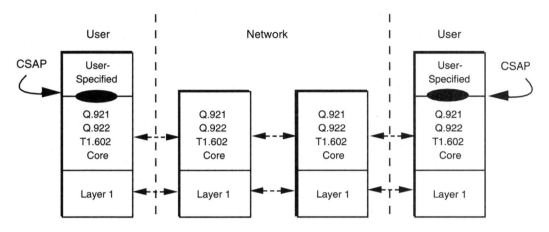

Figure 3–2 Core service access point (CSAP).

certain QOS features to see if they are being met in regard to the user's requested QOS. It must be able to provide congestion information to the core service user and it also must be able to provide some type of information about the release of the connection in the event of problems.

The OSI Model requires the use of primitive calls between the core service user and core service provider. These primitives are core data request and core data indication primitives and are mapped in operating system specific calls between the two software elements.

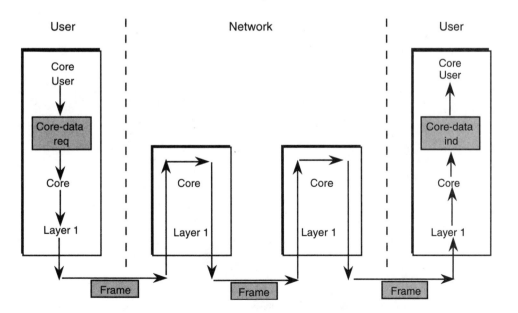

Figure 3–3 The primitives in the data transfer.

The core data request and indication primitives contain up to five parameters. These parameters are used to provide the transfer of the following information: The core service is provided through the use of service primitives and parameters. Two primitives are involved, the core data request and the core data indication. These primitives are passed between the core service user and core service provider. All primitives are passed as unconfirmed services. This means no confirmation is given the core service user that the core data has been accepted either by the service provider or by the peer user. No responses are provided either by the provider or by the other user.

Parameter Primitives

The service primitives contain up to five parameters: core user data, discard eligibility, congestion encountered backward, congestion encountered forward, and connection endpoint identifier (see Figure 3–4).

The core data parameter is used to convey data between the end users in the Frame Relay service. This data must be transferred in accordance with OSI's SDU (service data unit) concept, which means it must be transmitted without modification. The discard eligibility parameter is sent from the core service user to the service provider. It is used by the

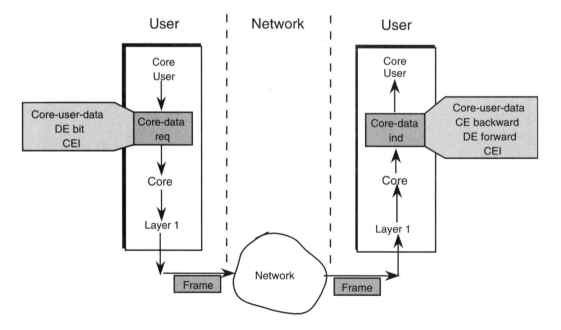

Figure 3–4   The parameters in the primitives.

provider to select CSDUs that may be discarded, assuming that the Frame Relay network decides that discarding is required.

The two congestion parameters are sent by the core data service provider to the core data service user to supply information about congestion that has been encountered in the network. The congestion encountered forward parameter is used to indicate that the provider has determined that congestion has occurred in transferring data to its user. The congestion backward parameter indicates that the provider has experienced congestion in transferring these units from the user.

The connection endpoint identifier parameter is used to further identity a connection endpoint. For example, this parameter would allow a DLCI to be used by more than one user and each user would be identified with a connection endpoint identifier value.

ONE SCENARIO FOR ATM FRAME RELAY INTERWORKING

Figure 3–5 provides an example of the ATM and Frame Relay internetworking operations. The interface between the Frame Relay entity and the AAL entity occurs through the Frame Relay core SAP (service access point) that is defined in the Frame Relay specifications. Therefore, the IWF must accommodate to the Frame Relay service definitions at this SAP. Ideally, the Frame Relay entity has no awareness of the AAL and ATM operations.

In accordance with the Frame Relay specifications, the service primitives contain up to five parameters: core user data, discard eligibility (DE), congestion encountered (CE) backward, congestion encountered (CE) forward, and connection endpoint identifier (CEI).

The *core user data* parameter is used to convey data between the end users in the Frame Relay service and is represented by FR-SSCS PDU. The DE parameter is sent from the core service user to the service provider (FR-SSCS) and is mapped into the ATM CLP bit.

The two congestion parameters supply information about congestion that is encountered in the network. The *congestion encountered forward* parameter is used to indicate that congestion has occurred in transferring data to the receiving user. The *congestion encountered backward parameter* indicates that the network has experienced congestion in transferring these units from the sending user.

The *connection endpoint identifier (CEI)* parameter is used to further identify a connection endpoint. For example, this parameter would

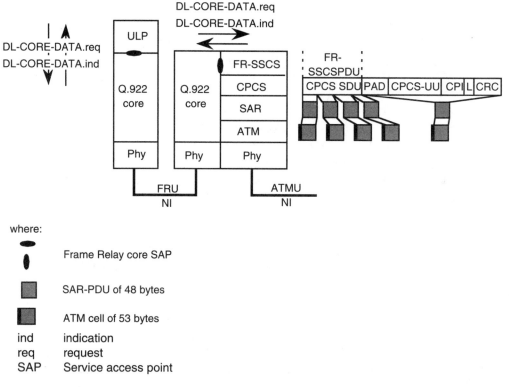

Figure 3–5   ATM and Frame Relay internetworking.

allow a DLCI to be used by more than one user and each user would be identified with a connection endpoint identifier value.

The AAL type 5 PDU is used to support Frame Relay and ATM interworking. As before, the CPI field is not yet defined. The CPCS-UU field is passed transparently by the ATM network. The length field is check for oversized or undersized PDUs. CRC violations are noted, and a reassembly timer can be invoked at the terminating endpoint.

GUIDANCE FROM RFC 1483

RFC 1483 defines two methods for carrying network interconnect traffic over an ATM network. The first method multiplexes multiple protocols over a single ATM virtual circuit. The second carries each protocol over a different ATM virtual circuit (VC). The gateway assumes the job of mapping functions between the Frame Relay network and the ATM network. At a minimum the following functions must be supported:

- *Variable length PDU formatting and delimiting:* Using AAL type 5, support the Frame Relay 2-octet control field (required), and the 3- and 4-octet control field (optional).
- *Error detection:* Using CRC-32, provide error detection over the FR PDU.
- *Connection multiplexing:* Associating one or multiple Frame Relay connections with one ATM VCC.
- *Loss priority indication:* Mapping the Frame Relay discard eligibility bit and the ATM cell loss priority bit.
- *Congestion indication:* Support of the Frame Relay forward and backward congestion notification features (within certain rules)

An FR-SSCS PDU consists of Frame Relay address field followed by an information field (I). The Frame Relay frame flags and the FCS are omitted, since the FCS functions are provided by the AAL, and the flag operations are supported by the underlying physical layer. Figure 3–6 shows an FR-SSCS-PDU encapsulated in the AAL5 CPCS PDU.

Routed and bridged traffic is carried inside the FR-SSCS-PDU as defined in RFC 1490. The protocol of the carried PDU is identified by prefixing the PDU by a network level protocol ID (NLPID).

The FR-SSCS supports variable length frames at the FR UNI over preestablished connections (PVCs). Each FR-SSCS connection is identified with a Frame Relay data link connection identifier (DLCI: equivalent to the ATM VPI/VCI). Multiple FR-SSCS connections can be associated with one Common Part CS (CPCS). The principal job of FR-SSCS is to emulate the FR UNI. In so doing, it supports Frame Relay forward and backward congestion notification (FECN, BECN), as well as the discard eligibility (DE) bit.

The CPCS is responsible for the following operations:

- Support of message mode (fixed-length blocks) or streaming mode (variable-length blocks) operations.
- Assured operations: CPCS is responsible for traffic integrity (retransmission of lost or corrupted PDUs.
- Non-assured operations: CPCS is not responsible for traffic integrity.

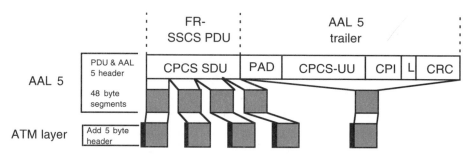

Note: CPCS PDU contains Q.922 header and user data.
where:

AAL   ATM adaptation layer
CPCS   Common part convergence sublayer
CPI   Common part identifier
CRC   Cyclic redundancy check
FR   Frame Relay
L   Length
PDU   Protocol data unit
RFC   Request for Comments
SSCS   Service specific part convergence sublayer
UU   User to user

Figure 3–6   RFC (Request for Comments) 1483.

The interface between the Frame Relay entity and the AAL entity occurs through the Frame Relay core SAP.

SUMMARY

The basic operations for internetworking Frame Relay and ATM were introduced in this chapter. These operations provide options for protocol encapsulation or protocol mapping and network interworking or service interworking.

The Frame Relay core service access point (CSAP) is a useful tool for the programmer in that it provides guidance on building an application programming interface (API) on top of the Frame Relay layers.

4

DXI and FUNI

In this chapter we examine the operations of the Data Exchange Interface (DXI) and the Frame User Network Interface (FUNI). We learn why DXI and FUNI were developed and cite the advantages and disadvantages of their use. A comparison is made of the DXI and FUNI headers in relation to the Frame Relay header. The role of the data service unit (DSU) is explained as well as the DXI and FUNI topologies.

WHY DXI AND FUNI WERE DEVELOPED

Until recently, there were few products that supported ATM interfaces and for the products that did exist, the ATM interface was quite expensive. In addition, some machines require significant architectural changes to support ATM operations.

The net effect was a reluctance to install ATM in end-user equipment. Notwithstanding these problems, the early ATM systems were viewed as effective candidates as basic backbone transport networks, yet there remained the problem of how to interface an end-user device into these ATM backbones. The DXI and FUNI standards were developed to address these issues and solve the problems just described. We can understand this statement better by examining the DXI and FUNI topologies.

DXI AND FUNI TOPOLOGIES

Figure 4–1 shows the topologies for DXI and FUNI. Figure 4–1a shows the DXI topology and Figure 4–1b shows the FUNI topology.

The DXI topology requires a data service unit (DSU, also known as channel service unit [CSU]) to rest between the user device and the ATM switch. This device provides several T1 functions such as the conversion of unipolar code to bipolar code, loopback testing, and other diagnostic operations. The DSU runs the ATM interface on the ATM side of the line, which relieves the end user from having to segment the traffic into cells and otherwise dealing with the cell technology.

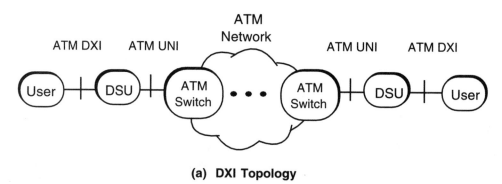

(a) DXI Topology

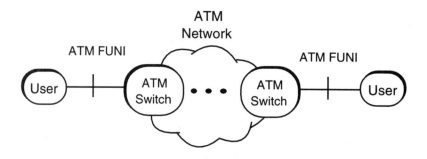

(b) FUNI Topology

Note: User device is usually a router and not a workstation/host.
where:
ATM   Asynchronous transfer mode
DSU   Data service unit
DXI   Data exchange interface
FUNI Frame UNI
UNI   User network interface

Figure 4–1   DXI and FUNI topologies.

Figure 4–1b shows the FUNI topology, in which the DSU is not required. The user runs its traffic directly between its device and the ATM switch. This approach is less expensive than the DXI option because the DSU is not necessary.

The FUNI interface is quite simple, as we will see later in this chapter. It requires a software setup between the user device and the ATM switch. Additionally, the FUNI payload (the I field) can be large (if necessary), which makes this interface attractive in relation to running the small cells across the communications line between the user and the ATM switch (as in the DXI option).

A LOOK AT THE HEADERS

Figure 4–2 depicts the structure and format of the Frame Relay UNI (FUNI) and Data Exchange Interface (DXI) headers. They are quite simi-

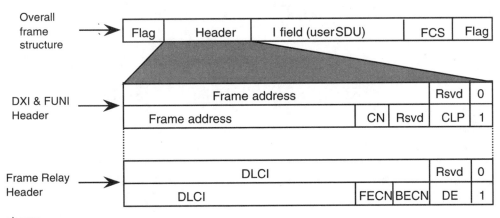

where:
  BECN   Backward explicit congestion notification bit
  C/R   Command/response bit
  CLP   Cell loss priority bit
  CN   Congestion notification bit
  DCLI   Data link connection identifier (10 bits)
  DE   Discard eligibility bit
  FCS   Frame check sequence (16 or 32 bits)
  FECN   Forward explicit congestion notification bit
  Rsvd   Reserved bit
  SDU   Service data unit (length varies)

Figure 4–2   Comparison of Frame Relay, Data Exchange Interface (DXI), and Frame UNI (FUNI) Headers.

lar to each other and the minor variations are explained here. First, notice that the header structure for DXI and FUNI are identical and the frame address for these two headers is in the same position as the Frame Relay DLCI. The command response (C/R) bit in the Frame Relay header is not instituted in DXI or FUNI, but is reserved for future use. The discard eligibility (DE) bit in the Frame Relay header is related to the DXI and FUNI cell loss priority (CLP) bit.

The Frame Relay BECN does not have a similar function in FUNI or DXI, or for that matter, it has no similar function in ATM either. As we learned earlier, the BECN is sent in the backward direction to indicate that traffic problems have occurred. The FECN bit of Frame Relay maps to the congestion notification (CN) bit of the DXI and FUNI headers, the FECN bit also maps to the CN bits in an ATM header. This information is forwarded to the recipient of the traffic, and it is assumed the destination end user will act upon these bits by sending some type of congestion notification to its sending user.

Finally, the CLP bit performs the same function as the DE bit, which is used for traffic tagging.

DXI MODES

DXI operates with three modes: Mode 1a is used only for AAL5, mode 1b operates with AAL3/4 and AAL5, and mode 2 operates with AAL3/4 and AAL5.

The principal differences between these modes lie in how many virtual connections are allowed across the interface and the size of the user payload (SDU) that is permitted. Additionally, each mode defines slightly different headers and trailers that are created by the DTE and/or DCE at the CPCS sublayer. Table 4–1 provides a summary of these modes.

EXAMPLE OF MODES 1A AND 1B

Figure 4–3 shows the relationship of the DTE layers and the DCE/SDU layers' modes 1a, 1b, and for AAL 5 traffic. The DTE DXI data link layer is closely related to an HDLC interface. Indeed, the use of HDLC-type frames eases the task of the DTE because HDLC is well known and implemented in many products. The task of the DTE is a relatively simple one to create a header that will provide enough information for the DCE to create a virtual circuit in the ATM network. In essence, the DXI header contains a DXI frame address (DFA), which is

Table 4–1   ATM Data Exchange Interface (DXI)

- *Mode 1a*
  Up to 1023 virtual connections
  AAL5 only
  Up to 9232 octets in DTE SDU
  16-bit FCS between DTE and DCE

- *Mode 1b*
  Up to 1023 virtual connections
  AAL3/4 for at least one virtual connection
  AAL5 for others
  Up to 9232 octets in DTE SDU for AAL5
  Up to 9224 octets in DTE SDU for AAL3/4
  16-bit FCS between DTE and DCE

- *Mode 2*
  Up to 16,777,215 virtual connections
  AAL5 and AAL3/4 (2^{24-1}): one per virtual connection
  Up to 65,535 (2^{16-1}) octets in DTE SDU
  32-bit FCS between DTE and DCE

used to convey the VPI and VCI values between the DTE and DCE. The DFA is 10 bits in length for modes 1a and 1b and 24 bits long in mode 2.

Figure 4–4 shows the activities for the support of AAL5 in modes 1a and 1b. The basic idea is to convey the DTE SDU across the ATM DXI to the DCE. The SDU is nothing more than the I field of the particular AAL protocol. This figure shows that the DTE encapsulates the DTE SDU into the DXI frame. The headers and trailers of this frame are then used by the DCE to receive the traffic and establish the virtual connection. The DCE is required to perform the ATM adaptation layer 5 common part

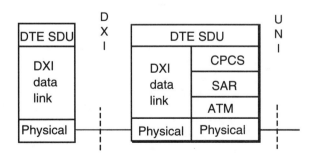

where:
  CPCS   Common part convergence sublayer
  SDU   Service data unit

Figure 4–3   Layers for modes 1a and 1b and AAL 5.

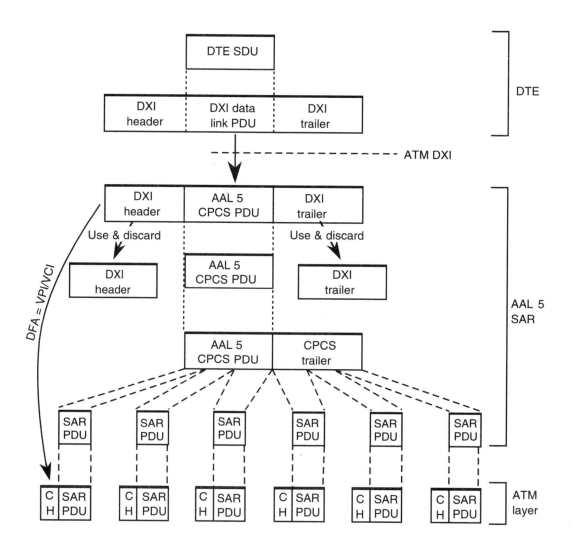

Notes:

The Frame Relay data link connection identifier in the DFA must be mapped into an ATM VPI/VCI.

The Frame Relay discard eligibility bit must be mapped to the ATM cell loss priority bit. Frame Relay congestion notification of FECN/BECN must be mapped into ATM congestion notification bits.

where:

BECN   Backward explicit congestion notification bit
DFA   DXI frame address
FECN   Forward explicit congestion notification bit

Figure 4–4   Modes 1a and 1b for AAL5.

convergence sublayer (AAL5 CPCS) as well as AAL segmentation and re-assembly operations (AAL5 SAR). The DCE also contains the ATM layer, which is responsible for the management of the cell header.

This specification does not define the operations of the service specific convergence sublayer, which is defined in ITU-T recommendation I.363.

EXAMPLES OF DXI FRAMES

Figure 4–5 shows examples of several of the frames transported across the DXI. Figure 4–5a illustrates modes 1a and 1b for AAL5. Figure 4–5b

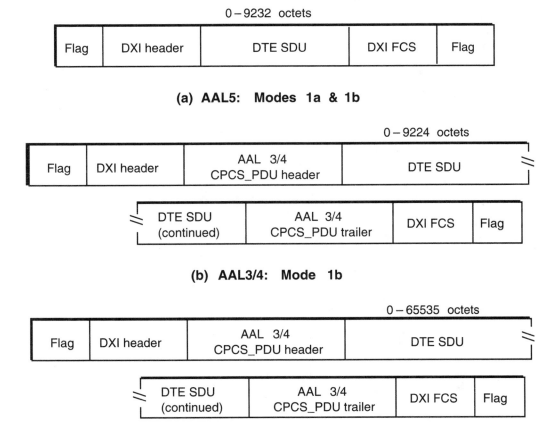

(a) AAL5: Modes 1a & 1b

(b) AAL3/4: Mode 1b

(c) Mode 2 data link frame

Figure 4–5   ATM DXI frames.

illustrates mode 1b with AAL3/4. The intent of the operations in Figures 4–5a and 4–5b is to emulate Frame Relay encapsulation, which, once again, requires few changes to the installed DTE devices in the industry. Finally, Figure 4–5c shows the contents of the mode 2 data link frame.

As Figure 4–6 shows, the DXI header and trailer are variations of the HDLC/LAPD header and trailer. The leading and trailing flags and the FCS fields are used in accordance with conventional HDLC operations. The DXI frame address (DFA) carries the bits for the VPI and VCI. Bits 6 through 3 of octet 1 represent the four least significant bits (LSBs) of the VPI. Bits 8 and 7 of octet 1 and bits 8 through 5 of octet 2 represent the six least significant bits of the VCI.

The four most significant bits (MSBs) of the VPI are set to 0 by the DCE on sending and ignored on receiving. Obviously, they are not coded in

Bit	8	7	6	5	4	3	2	1	Octet
Flag	0	1	1	1	1	1	1	0	0
DXI Header	DFA						RSVD	0	1
	DFA				CN	RSVD	CLP	1	2

(a) DXI Header

DXI Trailer	2^8	2^9	2^{10}	2^{11}	2^{12}	2^{13}	2^{14}	2^{15}	n–1
(FCS)	2^0	2^1	2^2	2^3	2^4	2^5	2^6	2^7	n
Flag	0	1	1	1	1	1	1	0	n+1

(b) DXI Trailer

where:
CLP   Cell loss priority
CN   Congestion notification
DFA   DXI frame address
FCS   Frame check sequence
RSVD   Reserved

Figure 4–6   DXI header and trailer for AAL5.

the DFA field. The ten MSBs of the VCI are set to 0 by the DCE on sending and ignored on receiving; they are not coded in the DFA field, either.

The congestion notification (CN) bit is used by the DCE if the last ATM cell that composes the DXI frame has the payload type identification (PTI) field set to 01x. The cell loss priority (CLP) bit is copied from the CLP bit sent from the DTE into the ATM cell header. The DCE does not see this bit when traffic is sent from the DCE to the DTE.

DXI FRAME ADDRESS MAPPINGS

Since DXI modes 1a and 1b restrict the number of virtual connections that can be established to 1023, 10 bits are sufficient for the VPI/VCI labels (2^{10-1} = 1023). And, since mode 2 permits 16,777,215 virtual connections, 24 bits are sufficient for the VPI/VCI (2^{24-1} = 16,777,215). Table 4–2 shows the mappings of the modes 1a and 1b 10-bit DFA and the mode 2 24–bit DFA to the VPI/VCI mappings.

COMPARISONS OF DXI AND FUNI

Table 4–3 provides a summary of the differences between DXI and FUNI. They are similar in their operations, but have some significant differences. FUNI is more flexible and does not require the installation of an SDU. It also allows the user of fractional T1.

For FUNI operations, the network is tasked with executing AAL to segment and reassemble the user's traffic. However, this arrangement allows the user link to/from the network to use frames and takes advantage of the variable (potentially large) information field in the frame. Thus, the overhead of the small payload in the ATM cell is not visible at the UNI. The network must absorb this overhead as part of its operations.

FRAME RELAY VS. DXI/FUNI

DXI and FUNI were developed as Frame Relay was maturing and becoming a major communications technology. Since Frame Relay is widely available, efficient and simple, this writer sees no compelling reason to use DXI or FUNI in place of Frame Relay, especially if it would mean the installation of another interface technology at the customer premises.

Table 4–2   DXI DFA Mappings to ATM VPI/VCI

Address Mapping	DFA Octet	DFA Bit	VPI Octet	VPI Bit	VCI Octet	VCI Bit
Modes 1A and 1B	1	6	2	8		
	1	5	2	7		
	1	4	2	6		
	1	3	2	5		
	1	8			3	2
	1	7			3	1
	2	8			4	8
	2	7			4	7
	2	6			4	6
	2	5			4	5
Mode 2	1	8	1	4		
	1	7	1	3		
	1	6	1	2		
	1	5	1	1		
	1	4	2	8		
	1	3	2	7		
	2	6	2	6		
	2	5	2	5		
	2	8			2	4
	2	7			2	3
	3	8			2	2
	3	7			2	1
	3	6			3	8
	3	5			3	7
	3	4			3	6
	3	3			3	5
	3	2			3	4
	4	8			3	3
	4	7			3	2
	4	6			3	1
	4	5			4	8
	4	4			4	7
	4	3			4	6
	4	2			4	5

Table 4–3 DXI and FUNI

DXI	FUNI
• DSU/CSU is required	• DSU/CSU is not required
• Cells still operate on the link	• Cells are created at the ATM switch
• Does not support Fractional T1	• Supports Fractional T1
• Does not supports SVCs	• Supports SVCs
• Supports SNMP	• Supports SNMP
• Uses a MIB	• Uses a MIB (a subset of the DXI MIB)
• Uses AAL 5 or 3/4	• Requires AAL5 with 3/4 optional
• Protocol encapsulation supported	• Protocol encapsulation supported

SUMMARY

We have seen that ATM can act as a transport mechanism for user multi-application traffic within and between networks and that ATM internetworking entails encapsulating user-network PDUs into the ATM cell through the invocation of AAL type 1, 3/4, and 5 modes. In addition, we've observed that the ATM DXI offloads some of the more complex AAL and ATM functions from a user device, while FUNI is based on DXI and provides a less complex and less expensive operation for the end user.

5

Network Interworking

This chapter describes the ATM Forum's Network Interworking specification, published as Document FRF.5. The emphasis is on how an ATM network is used to support transmission of traffic between Frame Relay systems. The network-interworking combinations are explained as well as the configuration options. The correlation of the Frame Relay quality of service features and those of ATM are also explored.

NETWORK INTERWORKING CONCEPTS

Figure 5–1 shows three Frame Relay service configurations for network A and network B through an ATM backbone. The configurations are labeled A1 through A3 for network A and B1 through B3 for network B. This is known as the Frame Relay internetworking scenario 1. It conforms to ITU-T I.555 (Frame Relay bearer service internetworking) and I.365.1 (Frame Relay service specific convergence sublayer, FR-SSCS). Several combinations of these interconnections are permitted. They are: (1) A1 to B1, (2) A1 to B2, (3) A1 to B3, (4) A2 to B2, (5) A2 to B3, and (6) A3 to B3.

ATM/Frame Relay network interworking does not stipulate any physical location for the interworking function (IWF). Figure 5–2 shows the possible placements of the IWF in relation to the access configura-

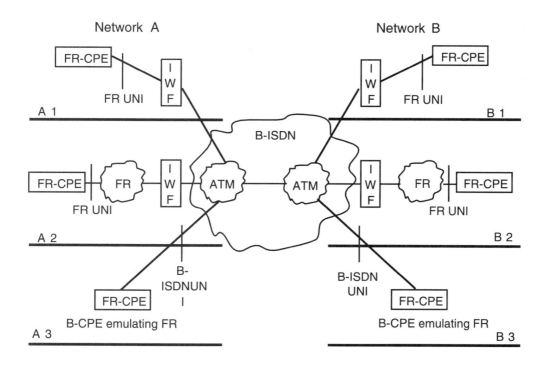

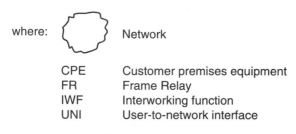

where: Network

CPE	Customer premises equipment
FR	Frame Relay
IWF	Interworking function
UNI	User-to-network interface

Figure 5–1   Network interworking topologies.

tions. Also, refer to Chapter 3, Figure 3–1. The IWF can be located at the Frame Relay network, the ATM network, at the customer premises equipment (CPE), or as a stand-alone unit, as in Figure 5–2a.

NETWORK INTERWORKING SCENARIOS

Figure 5–3 shows the structure and layers for interworking Frame Relay and ATM with what is known as scenario 1: the connection of two Frame Relay networks/CPE using B-ISDN. The interworking unit

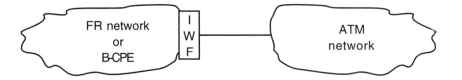

(a) Possible access configuration A2 or A3

(b) Possible access configuration A1 or A2

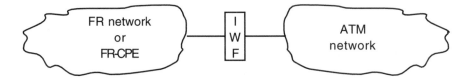

(c) Possible access configuration A1 or A2

where:
   CPE   Customer premise equipment
   FR   Frame Relay
   IWF   Interworking function

Figure 5–2   Configuration possibilities.

processes frames at the Frame Relay UNI with the user device using the Frame Relay Q.922 core procedures.

Scenario 1 supports the following reference configurations: A1–B1, A1–B2, A2–B2. Scenario 1 is also known as "Frame Relay Transport over ATM."

The IWF assumes the job of mapping functions between the Frame Relay network and the ATM network. The use of the B-ISDN network by the two Frame Relay networks/CPE is not visible to the end users. Therefore, the IWF must provide all mapping and encapsulation func-

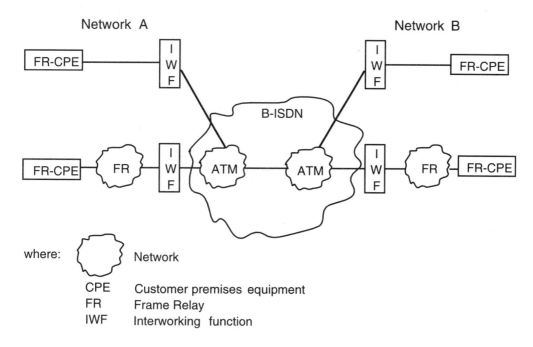

(a) **Reference configuration**

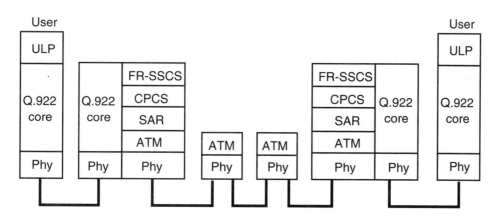

(b) **Protocol stacks**

where:
CPCS   Common part convergence sublayer
FR-SSCS Frame Relay service specific convergence sublayer

Figure 5–3   Network interworking scenario 1.

tions to ensure that the ATM presence does not change the end-to-end Frame Relay service.

The FR-SSCS (Frame Relay-service specific convergence sublayer) FR-SSCS supports variable length frames at the FR UNI over preestablished connections (PVCs). Each FR-SSCS connection is identified with a Frame Relay data link connection identifier (DLCI: equivalent to the ATM VPI/VCI). Multiple FR-SSCS connections can be associated with one Common Part CS (CPCS).

The principal job of FR-SSCS is to emulate the FR UNI. In so doing, it supports Frame Relay forward and backward congestion notification (FECN, BECN), as well as the discard eligibility (DE) bit.

The CPCS is responsible for the following operations:

- Support of message mode (fixed-length blocks) or streaming mode (variable-length blocks) operations.
- Nonassured operations: CPCS is not responsible for traffic integrity.

For scenario 1, the use of the B-ISDN network is not visible to the end users, which means the end user protocols are not impacted. The IWF is responsible for encapsulation and mapping the end users' traffic in a transparent manner.

Scenario 1 supports the following network internetworking configurations: (1) A1 to B1, (2) A1 to B2, and (3) A2 to B2.

The second scenario for network internetworking is scenario 2, which requires the B-ISDN CPE to support the Frame Relay service specific convergence sublayer (FR-SSCS) (see Figure 5–4). In this scenario, the use of ATM and B-ISDN must not be visible to the Frame Relay end user.

The reference configurations that must be supported by scenario 2 are A1 to B3 and A2 to B3. For this scenario, the reference configuration of A3 to B3 is not discussed in the ITU-T I.555.

NETWORK INTERWORKING FUNCTIONS

The Frame Relay/ATM network interworking specification defines six network interworking functions that are based on the ATM Forum B-ICI (Broadband Intercarrier Interface) specification. These functions are as follows (and each is explained in the following material):

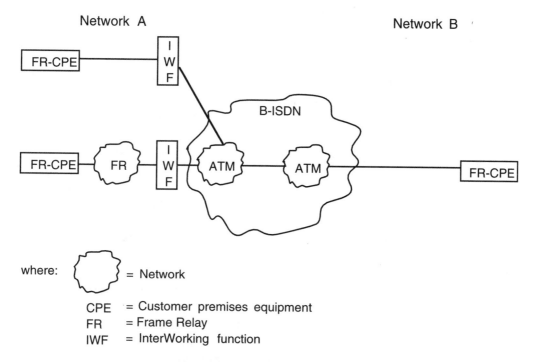

(a) Reference configuration

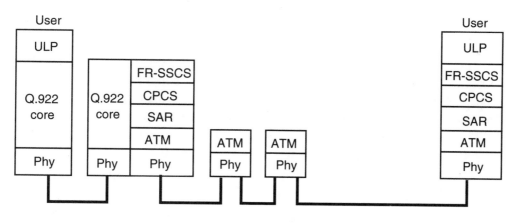

(b) Protocol stacks

where:
CPCS   Common part convergence sublayer
FR-SSCS   Frame Relay service specific convergence sublayer

Figure 5–4   Network interworking scenario 2.

- Variable length PDU formatting and delimiting
- Error detection
- Connection multiplexing
- Discard eligibility and cell Loss priority mapping
- Congestion indication (forward and backward)
- PVC status management

Variable Length PDU Formatting and Delimiting

The network interworking function supports variable length PDUs. The convention is to accept a PDU format that is identical to the Frame Relay Q.922 core PDU less the flags, the FCS field, and the zero bit insertion operation. This is the type of PDU that is expected by FR-SSCS. The FR/ATM IWF must use the FR-SSCS in accordance with ITU-T I.365.1 and the PDU formats shown as shown in Figure 5–5. The FR/ATM IWF must also use the AAL5 CPCS and SAR in accordance with ITU-T I.363.

As shown in Figure 5–5, the system must support the 2-octet format, whereas the 3-octet format is for further study and the 4-octet format is optional. Notice that the address extension bit (EA) is set to 0 to indicate that the header is extended one more octet.

Error Detection

Figure 5–6 shows the relationship of the FR-SSCS PDU to the CP-AAL5 and the ATM layers. AAL5 performs its conventional segmentation and reassembly functions by delineating the traffic into 48-byte data units with the addition of an 8-byte trailer as part of the last data unit.

The error detection operation is provided by the AAL5 CRC-32 calculation over the FR-SSCS PDU.

Connection Multiplexing

It may be desirable to map multiple Frame Relay connections to a single ATM connection. For the networking interworking specification, the FR-SSCS must support connection multiplexing on either a one-to-one basis (a single FR connection is mapped to a single ATM connection) or many-to-one basis (multiple FR connections are mapped to a single ATM connection). In both cases, a correlation must be made between the Frame Relay data link connection identifier (DLCI) and the ATM virtual path identifier/virtual channel identifier (VPI/VCI). These operations are

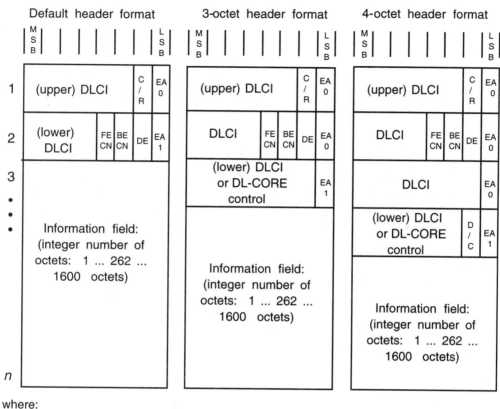

where:
- BECN Backward explicit congestion notification bit
- C/R Command/response bit
- D/C DLCI or DL-CORE control indicator
- DE Discard eligibility bit
- DLCI Data link connection identifier
- EA Address extension bit
- FECN Forward explicit congestion notification bit

Figure 5–5 Variable length PDU formatting and delimiting.

also described in ITU-T I.555. Let us now examine the two modes of connection multiplexing (see Figures 5–7 and 5–8).

One-to-One Multiplexing.   For the case of one-to-one multiplexing, the multiplexing is performed at the ATM layer using ATM VPIs/VCIs. The Frame Relay DLCIs can range from 16 to 991 and the values must be agreed upon between the ATM end systems (that is to say, IWFs or ATM end users). Otherwise, a default value of 1022 will be used for the operation. These rules apply for 2-octet Frame Relay header. If 3- or

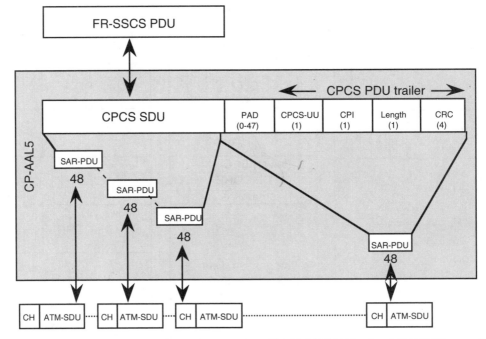

Note: Error detection is provided over the complete FR-SSCS PDU for the AAL5 CRC operation
where:

ATM	Asynchronous transfer mode
CH	Cell header
CP-AAL5	Common part ATM adaptation layer type 5
CPCS SDU	Common part convergence sublayer service data unit
CPCS-UU	CPCS user to user
CPI	Common part indicator
CRC	Cyclic redundancy check
FR-SSCS	Frame Relay service specific convergence sublayer
SAR PDU	Segmentation and reassembly protocol data unit

Figure 5–6   FR-CPCS operations (including error detection).

4-octet headers are used, the DLCI value must be agreed upon between
the two ATM end systems and the standards do not specify a default
value.

Many-to-One Multiplexing.   For the case of the many-to-one multiplexing, the Frame Relay connections are multiplexed into a single ATM
virtual channel connection (VCC) and identification of the Frame Relay
traffic is achieved by using multiple DLCIs. The many-to-one operation

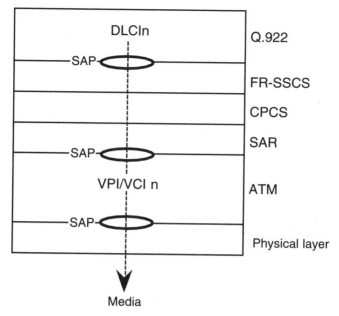

where:

ATM	Asynchronous transfer mode
CPCS	Common part convergence sublayer
DLCI	Data link connection identifier
FR-SSCS	Frame Relay service specific convergence sublayer
SAP	Service access point
SAR	Segmentation and reassembly
VCI	Virtual channel identifier
VPI	Virtual path identifier

Figure 5–7 Connection multiplexing (one-to-one).

is restricted to Frame Relay connections that terminate on the same ATM-based system.

The specification has no rules on the DLCI values that are to be used. Therefore, they must be agreed upon between the two ATM end systems.

Discard Eligibility and Cell Loss Mapping

The IWF equipment must support two modes of operation for discard eligibility and cell loss priority bit mapping (see Table 5–1). Be aware that these modes operate in the Frame Relay to B-ISDN direction.

For mode 1, the discard eligibility (DE) bit in the Frame Relay frame header must be copied without alteration into the DE bit that is coded in

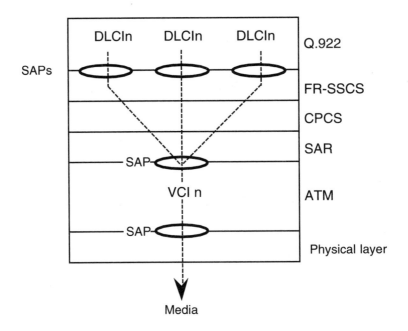

Media

where:

ATM	Asynchronous transfer mode
CPCS	Common part convergence sublayer
DLCI	Data link connection identifier
FR-SSCS	Frame Relay service specific convergence sublayer
SAP	Service access point
SAR	Segmentation and reassembly
VCI	Virtual channel identifier
VPI	Virtual path identifier

Figure 5–8   Connection multiplexing (many-to-one).

**Table 5–1   Discard Eligibility and Cell Loss Mapping
(Frame Relay to B-ISDN Direction)**

Mode 1:

- Discard eligibility bit (DE) if Frame Relay frame header copied into DE bit of FR-SSCS header

- Then, copied into cell loss priority bit (CLP) of each ATM cell header created in the segmentation process

Mode 2:

- Discard eligibility bit (DE) if Frame Relay frame header copied into DE bit of FR-SSCS header

- Then ATM CLP bit is set to a constant value of 0 or 1

- This constant value is determined at setup time, and must remain unchanged

---

the FR-SSCS header. Next, this bit must be mapped into the cell loss priority (CLP) bit in the header of each ATM cell that is generated as a result of segmenting each specific Frame Relay frame.

For mode 2, the DE bit in the Frame Relay frame header must be copied without alteration into the DE bit in the FR-SSCS header and the ATM CLP bit shall be set to a constant value of 0 or 1. This value is decided when the connection is set up and must be used for all cells generated from the segmentation process for every frame. It must remain unchanged until such time that a ATM connection has its characteristics changed.

To support discard eligibility (DE) and cell loss priority (CLP) mapping in the B-ISDN to Frame Relay mapping, the network provider can choose between two modes of operations. For mode 1, if one or more ATM cells pertaining to a segmented frame has its CLP bit set to 1, or if the DE bit of the FR-SSCS PDU is set to 1, then the IWF must set the DE bit to 1 of the Frame Relay frame. For mode 2, the FR-SSCS PDU DE bit is copied without alteration into the Q.922 DE bit. This operation is independent of any cell loss priority indications received by the ATM layer. Figure 5–9 summarizes these modes of operation with four tables.

FR-to-ATM (Mode 1)			FR-to-ATM (Mode 2)			ATM-to-FR (Mode 1)			ATM-to-FR (Mode 2)		
fromQ.922 Core	mapped toFR-SSCS	mapped to ATM layer	fromQ.922 Core	mapped toFR-SSCS	mapped toATM layer	fromATM layer	fromFR-SSCS	toQ.922 Core	fromATM layer	fromFR-SSCS	toQ.922 Core
DE	DE	CLP	DE	DE	CLP	CLP	DE	DE	CLP	DE	DE
0	0	0	0	0	Y	0	0	0	X	0	0
1	1	1	1	1	Y	1	X	1	X	1	1
						X	1	1			
Note 1			Note 2			Note 3					

Note 1: For all cells generated from the segmentation process of that frame.
Note 2: Y can be 0 or 1.
Note 3: For one-or-more cells of the frame, X indicates that the value does not matter (0 or 1).

Figure 5–9   Discard eligibility and cell loss mapping (B-ISDN to Frame Relay direction).

Congestion Indication

The congestion indication function is organized as follows:

Congestion indication (forward):
Frame Relay-to-B-ISDN direction
B-ISDN-to-Frame Relay direction

Congestion indication (backward):
Frame Relay-to-B-ISDN direction
B-ISDN-to-Frame Relay direction

The forward congestion indication is supported with the Frame Relay FECN bit and the ATM forward congestion indication bit. For the Frame Relay to B-ISDN direction, the FECN bit in the frame header must be copied unchanged into the FECN field of the FR-SSCS PDU. The ATM forward congestion indication bit must always be set to congestion not experienced.

For the B-ISDN-to-Frame Relay direction, the forward congestion indication bit in the last ATM cell of the segmented frame received must be set to congestion experienced. However, if the FECN bit of the received FR-SSCS PDU is set to congestion experienced, then the IWF must set the FECN bit in the Frame Relay frame header.

The rules for the use of the congestion indication (forward) operations are summarized in Figure 5–10.

FR-to-ATM			ATM-to-FR		
Q.922F ECN	SSCSFE CN	ATMEF CI	ATMEF CI	SSCSFE CN	Q.922F ECN
0	0	0	0	0	0
1	1	0	X	1	1
			1	X	1

Note: 0 indicates congestion is not experienced
1 indicates congestion is experienced
x indicates that the value does not matter (0 or 1)

where:
0 indicates congestion is not experienced
1 indicates congestion is experienced
X indicates that the value does not matter (0 or 1)

Figure 5–10   Congestion indication (forward).

As a general rule, the backward congestion indication operation is supported only by the Frame Relay BECN bit.

For the B-ISDN-to-Frame Relay direction, the BECN bit in the FR-SSCS PDU must be copied unchanged into the BECN bit of the Frame Relay frame header.

For the Frame Relay-to-B-ISDN direction, two conditions must be met if the BECN bit in the FR-SSCS PDU is set to congestion experienced by the IWF. These conditions are:

- The BECN bit is set in the frame header relayed in the Frame Relay- to-B-ISDN direction or
- The ATM forward congestion indication bits were set to congestion experienced in the last ATM cell of the last segmented frame that was received in the B-ISDN-to-Frame Relay direction.

The Frame Relay Forum document specification number FRF.5 and the B-ICI provide a state diagram to describe the operations to exit the congestion state depending on the activity of the ATM virtual channel. In

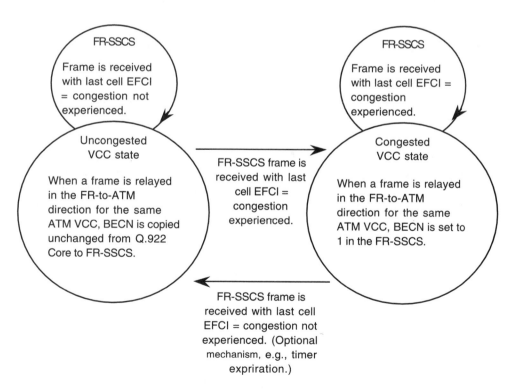

Figure 5–11   Congestion state diagram.

essence, Figure 5–11 shows that a timer can be used to reset a congestion state if no new congestion information is received in the B-ISDN-to-Frame Relay direction. The state diagram establishes that the congestion state must be cleared if the ATM forward congestion indication bits of the last cell in the next frame received is not set. If this event does not occur, the timer is restarted.

PVC Status Management

The network interworking for PVC management is based on the ATM Forum B-ICI specification. The basic idea is to allow the PVC ATM layer and the Frame Relay PVC status management of the FR-SSCS layer to operate independently of each other, as shown in Figure 5–12. This approach recognizes the difficulty of correlating management functions between two different protocols.

In essence, the individual management of Frame Relay PVCs at the Frame Relay UNI and Frame Relay NNI does not change. This operation only covers the management of the Frame Relay PVCs carried through the ATM network, which is stipulated in ITU-T Q.933 Annex A. These operations can consist of all six reference configurations described earlier in this chapter (A1–A3, B1–B3).

In addition, PVC management must adhere to ITU-T Q.933 Annex A, but with four changes: (1) the N391 counter default value is 1, (2) the T391 timer default value is 180 seconds, (3) the T392 timer default value is 200 seconds, and (4) the Frame Relay asynchronous message usage is recommended.

Rules for Multiprotocol Encapsulation.
User protocols (upper layer protocols or ULPs) can be encapsulated into the Frame Relay information field based on the Frame Relay Forum Multiprotocol Encapsulation specification (FRF.3). This specification is based on the Internet RFC 1490 and ANSI T1.617a Annex F. This operation is centered around ISO/IEC TR49577, more commonly known as the network layer protocol id (NLPID). Chapter 2 provides information on the encapsulation operations and RFC 1490.

SUMMARY

Network interworking provides two scenarios, 1 and 2. With scenario 1, two Frame Relay networks/CPE are connected using B-ISDN. The interworking unit processes frames at the Frame Relay UNI with

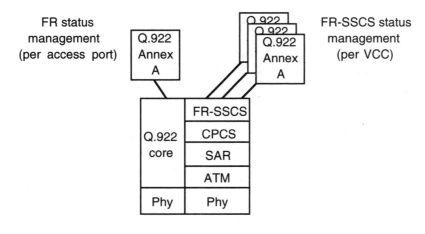

(a) At the IWF

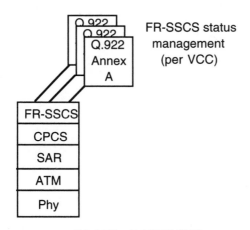

(b) At the B-ISDN CPE

where:
ATM	Asynchronous transfer mode
CPCS	Common part convergence sublayer
DLCI	Data link connection identifier
FR-SSCS	Frame Relay service specific convergence sublayer
SAP	Service access point
SAR	Segmentation and reassembly
VCC	Virtual channel connection

Figure 5–12   Permanent virtual circuit (PVC) status management.

the user device using the Frame Relay Q.922 core procedures. Scenario 1 supports the following reference configurations: A1–B1, A1–B2, A2–B2. Scenario 1 is also known as "Frame Relay Transport over ATM."

Scenario 2 requires the B-ISDN CPE to support the Frame Relay service specific convergence sublayer (FR-SSCS). In this scenario, the use of ATM and B-ISDN must not be visible to the Frame Relay end user.

6

Service Interworking

This chapter describes the ATM Forum's Service Interworking specification, published as Document FRF.8. The emphasis is on how an ATM network is used to support transmission of traffic between Frame Relay and ATM systems. The network-interworking combinations are explained as well as the configuration options. The correlation of the Frame Relay quality of service features and those of ATM are also explored.

DEFINITIONS OF SERVICE INTERWORKING

As introduced in Chapter 1, service interworking is similar to network interworking, but the ATM service user has no knowledge of the remote Frame Relay system. The Frame Relay service user performs no ATM services and the ATM service user performs no Frame Relay services. All interworking operations between the user are performed by the IWF.

Figure 6–1 shows the structure of service interworking and the protocol stacks. The location of the IWF is not dictated by any standard and can be placed in a single node or multiple nodes, depending upon the specific topology of an interworking environment.

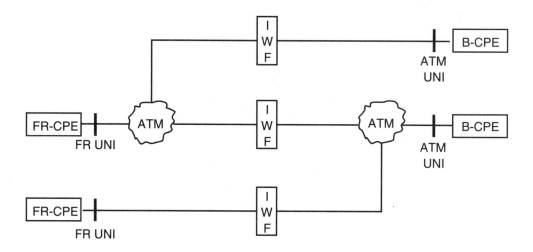

(a) Configuration

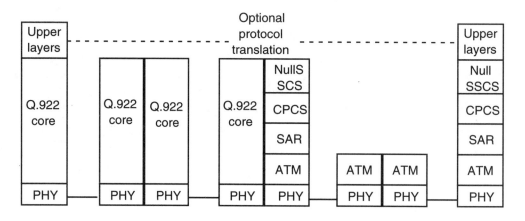

(b) Protocol stacks

where:

ATM	Asynchronous transfer mode
B-CPE	Broadband customer premise equipment (ATM-based)
CPCS SDU	Common part convergence sublayer service data unit
CPCS-UU	CPCS user to user
IWU	Interworking unit
PHY	Physical layer
SAR	Segmentation and reassembly
SSCS	Service specific convergence sublayer
UNI	User network interface

Figure 6–1   Service Interworking.

The B-ISDN service user (labeled the B-CPE in the figure) uses B-ISDN class C AAL5 operations with message mode, and unassured operations. AAL5 SAR is used, as well as AAL5 CPCS, and a null SSCS.

FR-ATM INTERWORKING SERVICE

As shown in Figure 6–2, the FR-ATM interworking service is provided through a combination of the FR-ATM IWF at the ATM network edge and a series of ATM interfaces (hops) to the remote ATM network edge. The service characteristics of the FR-ATM connection are a combination of the service characteristics of the FR-ATM IWF and the FR UNI. The FR-ATM IWF (through the FR UNI functionality) is connected to either a third-party Frame Relay network or CPE (both of which are external to the ATM network).

Frames are identified at the Frame Relay interface through the 10-bit data link connection identifier (DLCI), which is an identifier with local significance only. The DLCI permits multiple logical connections to

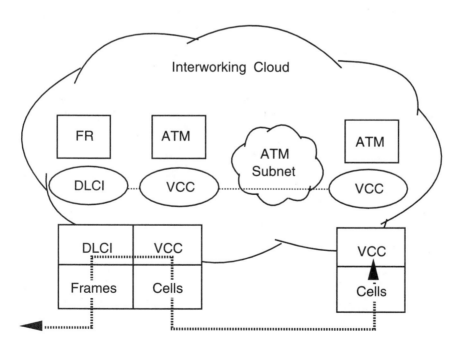

Figure 6–2   Frame Relay-ATM interworking cloud.

many destinations over a single access channel. Frames belonging to each logical connection are identified by distinct DLCI values and are correlated with an ATM VCC.

SERVICE INTERWORKING FUNCTIONS

The FR-ATM IWF operation must support a bearer service that is order-preserving, reliable, and operating with best-effort delivery of frames from the network edge of the FR UNI to the network edge of the ATM connection point.

For each connection in the user data transfer protocol stack (U-plane), the bearer service has the following operating characteristics:

- Provides bidirectional transfer of frames
- Preserves the frame order as given at the UNI upon delivery to the ATM network or end-point
- Detects transmission, format, and operational errors
- Provides transparent transport for each frame's user data contents; only the administrative (including the address and the frame check sequence [FCS]) fields are modified
- Does not acknowledge frames
- Does not retransmit frames

The FR-ATM interworking service supports ANSI T1.606 Addendum1:

- Compliance with the standard implementation of committed information rate (CIR), committed burst (Bc), excess burst (Be), and discard eligibility (DE)
- Forward explicit congestion notification (FECN) and backward explicit congestion notification (BECN) congestion signaling
- Frame discard preference under congestion

Table 6–1 lists the Frame Relay service I.233.1 Core Functions and correlates these functions to the B-ISDN Class, Message Mode, unassured operations. For this mode, the table lists the ATM functions and the AAL5 SAR and CPCS functions.

Table 6–1   Comparison of Functions in FR-ATM Service Interworking

Frame Relay Service		B-ISDN Class C, Message Mode, Unassured	
I.233.1 Core Functions	*ATM Functions*	*SAR and CPCS Function (AAL5)*
Frame delimiting, alignment, and transparency		Preservation of CPCS-SDU
Frame muxing/demuxing using the DLCI field	Muxing/demuxing using VPI/VCI	
Inspection of the frame to ensure that it is neither too long or too short		
Detection of (but not recovery from) transmission errors		Detection of (but not recovery from) transmission errors
Congestion control forward	Congestion control forward	
Congestion control backward		
Command/response		CPCS-UU
Congestion control discard eligibility	Cell loss priority	

The B-ISDN service is sparse. This intent is to provide few services in order to improve efficiency. Of course, since the SSCS in null in this stack, there are not a lot of operations that the AAL5 can execute.

The Frame Relay/ATM service interworking specification defines four network interworking functions that are based on the ATM Forum B-ICI (Broadband Intercarrier Interface) specification. These functions are as follows:

- Frame formatting and delimiting
- Discard eligibility and cell loss priority mapping
- Congestion indication
- Mapping the DLCI

This section of the chapter provides a summary of these four operations and Table 6–2 provides a summary of this discussion.

Table 6–2   Service Interworking Functions

- Frame formatting and delimiting
  FR-to-ATM: FR fame mapped to AAL5 PDU, with flags, stuffed bits, and FCS
    removed. Some of the Q.922 fields are mapped to ATM header
  ATM-FR: The opposite operations occur
- Discard eligibility and cell loss priority mapping
  FR-to-ATM:
    Mode 1: Discard eligibility bit (DE) in the Frame Relay frame header mapped to
      ATM CLP bit of every cell of the SAR operation
    Mode 2: ATM CLP bits are set to a constant value of 0 or 1
  ATM-to-FR:
    Mode 1: If one or more cells has CLP bit set, DE bit is also set
    Mode 2: DE bit must be a constant value configured at set up time
- Congestion indication forward
  FR-to-ATM:
    Mode 1: FECN bit mapped to the ATM explicit forward congestion indication
      (EFCI) field of every cell generated from the SAR operation
    Mode 2: FECN field is not mapped to the ATM EFCI field, but set to a constant
      value of "congestion not experienced"
  ATM-to-FR:
    ATM EFCI field (congestion or not congestion) is set to the FECN bit of the Frame
      Relay frame header
    Congestion indication backward
  FR-to-ATM:
    BECN bit is ignored
  ATM-to-FR:
    BECN bit is always set to 0
- Mapping the DLCI
  A one to one mapping is always made between DLCIs and VPI/VCIs

Frame Formatting and Delimiting

Frame formatting and delimiting differs depending on the direction of the traffic flow. For the Frame Relay to ATM direction, the frame is mapped into an AAL5 PDU. During this operation, the frame flags and FCS field are stripped away and any bit stuffing operations are reversed. Additionally, the Frame Relay header is removed with some of its fields mapped into the ATM cell header fields.

For the ATM-to-Frame Relay direction, AAL5's message delineation capability is used to align frame boundaries for the bit stuffing operations to occur. In addition, flags and the FCS field are inserted and the encapsulation fields are translated into the protocol fields of the frame.

Discard Eligibility and Cell Loss Priority Mapping

The operations described for discard eligibility and cell loss priority mapping are organized in the Frame Relay-to-ATM direction and the ATM-to-Frame Relay direction. In both directions, two modes of operation are supported.

For the Frame Relay-to-ATM direction, mode 1 must be supported with mode 2 provisioned as an option. If both modes are supported in the IWF equipment, they must be configurable on a specific virtual connection basis.

In the mode 1 operation, the Frame Relay DE bit is mapped to the ATM CLP bit in every cell generated by the segmentation process. In the mode 2 operation, the DE bit of the frame header is set to a constant value. The value is configured on a PVC basis at subscription time.

For the ATM-to-Frame Relay direction, two modes of operations also are permitted with mode 1 required and mode 2 optional. Once again, if both modes are available, each must be configurable per virtual connection.

In the mode 1 operation, if at least one cell belonging to a frame has its CLP bit set, the IWF must set the DE bit of the resulting Frame Relay frame. In the mode 2 operation, the DE bit of the frame is set to a constant value. The value is configured on a PVC basis at subscription time.

Congestion Indication

Congestion Indication Forward.   In the Frame Relay to ATM direction, two modes of operation can be selected for mapping forward congestion indication. In mode 1, the FECN bit in the Frame Relay frame header is mapped to the ATM explicit forward congestion indication (EFCI) field of every cell generated from the SAR operation. In mode 2, the FECN field of the Frame Relay frame header is not mapped to the ATM EFCI field. The EFCI field is set to a constant value of "congestion not experienced."

In the ATM to Frame Relay direction, the ATM EFCI field (congestion or not congestion) is set to the FECN bit of the Frame Relay frame header.

Congestion Indication Backward (BECN has no equivalent function in AAL5 or ATM).   In the Frame Relay-to-ATM direction, the BECN bit is ignored. In the ATM-to-Frame Relay direction, the BECN bit is always set to 0.

Mapping the DLCI

Finally, a one-to-one mapping between Frame Relay DLCIs and ATM VPI/VCIs always occurs in service interworking.

PVC MANAGEMENT PROCEDURES

UTU-T Recommendation Q.933, Annex A defines the PVC management procedures. For service interworking, these procedures must be bidirectional, with the support of asynchronous operations optional.

The ATM Forum UNI and B-ICI specifications establish the procedures for PVC management on the ATM side of the IWF. The IWF is tasked with mapping the alarms from Frame Relay to ATM and from ATM to Frame Relay.

Figure 6–3 shows the configurations for PVC management operations and lists the PVC management procedures. Volume 1 of this series provides information on these operations.

FORMATTING AND IDENTIFICATION PROCEDURES

Figure 6–4 shows the formatting and identification conventions for the interworking of Frame Relay frames with the AAL5 CPCS PDUs. The frame and the PDU use the ongoing standards (RFC 1483, Chapter 2) for these operations. They are:

Control: The control field, as established in High Level Data Link Control (HDLC) standards

NLPID: The network level protocol id, as established in the ISO/IEC TR 9577 standard

OUI: The organization unique id, as established in RFCs 826, 1042, and several others

LLC: The logical link protocol, as established in the IEEE 802.x standards

Bridged PDUs

Figure 6–5 shows the conventions for header translation of the local area network (LAN) 802.3, 802.4, 802.5, and FDDI protocol data units

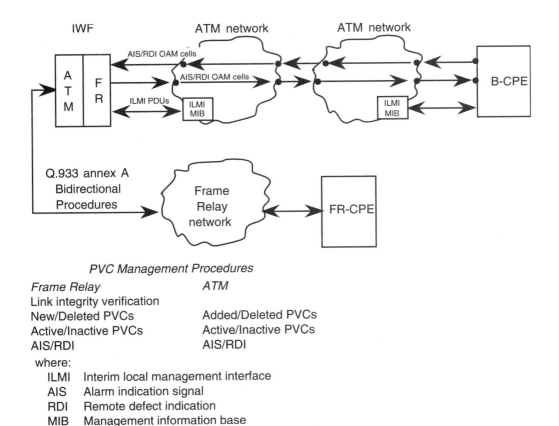

Figure 6–3 PVC management operations.

(PDUs). The NLPID header is set to 0x80, which indicates a SNAP header follows.

These PDUs are called bridged PDUs, because they are encapsulated using the SNAP OUI field of 0x00-80-C2, which is a reserved value for this type of encapsulation (OUI = 0x00-80-C2 is reserved for IEEE 802.1 encapsulation).

The PID part of the SNAP header identifies the type of LAN traffic that is encapsulated. These values indicate the presence of 802.3, 802.4, 802.5, or FDDI traffic as follows:

Preserved FCS	FCS not preserved	LAN type
0x00-01	0x00-07	802.3/Ethernet*
0x00-02	0x00-08	802.4
0x00-03	0x00-09	802.5
0x00-04	0x00-0A	FDDI
0x00-05	0x00-0B	802.6

* Ethernet cited in RFC 1294

The AAL5 CPCS-PDU header contains the logical link control (LLC) header of destination service access point (DSAP), which is set to 0xAA (170_{10}); source SAP (SSAP), which is also set to 0xAA (170_{10}); and the conventional HDLC control field, which is set to 0x03. The coding of 0xAA-AA is reserved in LLC to indicate that a SNAP header is present.

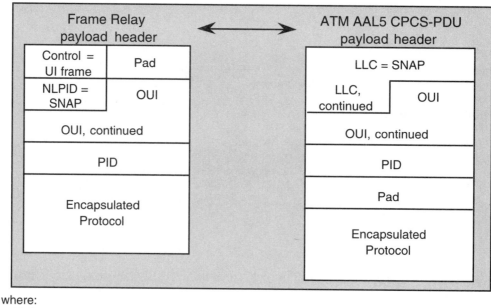

where:

LLC	Logical link control
NLPID	Network level protocol id
OUI	Organization unique id
Pad	Align to a 2-octet boundary (optional)
PID	Protocol id
SNAP	Subnetwork access protocol
UI	Unnumbered acknowledgment frame

Figure 6–4 Formatting and identification conventions.

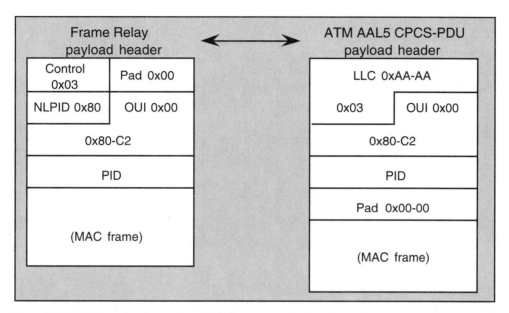

Note: RFC 1483 (multiprotocol encapsulation over AAL5) defines the encapsulation of Ethernet with an OUI of 0x00-00-00, followed by the Ethertype field.
where:

Term		Meaning of hex values coded above
LLC	Logical link control	Presence of SNAP header
NLPID	Network level protocol id	Presence of SNAP header
SNAP	Subnetwork access protocol	The OUI and PID fields
OUI	Organization unique id	Bridged PDUs (0x00-80-C2)
PID	Protocol id	Type of traffic and FCS use—see text

Figure 6–5   Header translation for bridged PDUs (IEEE 802.3, 802.4, 802.5, 802.6, FDDI).

Bridges and Source-Routed PDUs.   The conventions cited above are quite similar to those used to encapsulate Bridge PDUs (BPDUs) and source-routed BPDUs. For the former, the PID is 0x00-0E. For the latter, the PID is 0x00-0F.

Routed IP PDUs.   For the encapsulation of IP datagrams, the NLPID in the Frame Relay payload header of 0xCC (the reserved NLPID value for IP) is mapped to/from the PID value of 0x08-00 (the reserved PID value for IP) (see Figure 6–6).

In the AAL5 CPCS-PDU payload header, the OUI is set to 0x00-00-00.

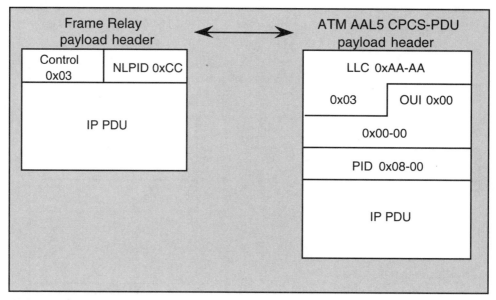

Note: Mapping is performed between the Frame Relay payload header of 0xCC (the reserved NLPID value for IP) and the PID value of 0x08-00 (the reserved PDI value for IP).

Figure 6–6   Frame Relay /ATM payload header for routed IP PDUs.

Routed OSI PDUs

The operations of encapsulation should be understood by now. The next few examples are based on the previous discussions and use some reserved NLPIDs and LLC SAPs to identify other types of traffic. Figure 6–7 shows the conventions for header translation of routed OSI PDUs.

Other Encapsulations

Figure 6–8 shows the procedure for encapsulation of X.25/ISO 8202 packets.

As a final example, Figure 6–9 shows the relationship of the Frame Relay and AAL5 header translations for the signaling procedures (switched virtual calls, or connections on demand).

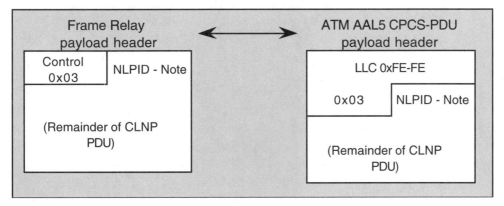

Note: Allowed NLPID values are 0x81, 0x82, and 0x83.
where:

0x81   identifies connectionless network protocol (CLNP) traffic
0x82   identifies end-system to intermediate system (ES-IS) traffic
0x83   identifies intermediate system to intermediate system (IS-IS) traffic

Figure 6–7   Frame Relay /ATM payload header for routed OSI PDUs.

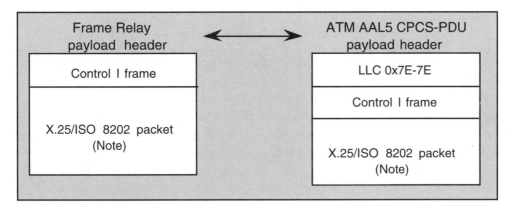

Note: The first octet identifies the NLPID.

Figure 6–8   Frame Relay /ATM payload header for X.25/ISO 8208 packets.

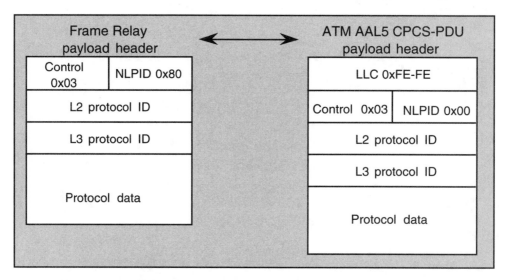

Figure 6–9   Frame Relay /ATM payload translation for Q.931, Q.933, or Q.2931 protocols.

ARP PROCEDURES

Chapter 2 introduced the Address Resolution Protocol (ARP). It is published as RFC 826, and Inverse ARP is published as RFC 1293. Frame Relay uses RFC 1490 and ATM uses RFC 1577 for ARP-type operations.

FRF.8 provides the specific configuration for ARP operations, and defines the responsibility of the IWF to support ARP mapping (see Figure 6–10). The IWF uses a mapping table to correlate the Frame Relay and ATM virtual circuit labels. The table contains the following information:

- Frame Relay port number on IWF interface P1
- Frame Relay DLCI value on this port (notation ee in the figure)
- ATM port number on IWF interface P2
- ATM VPI/VCI values on this port (notation aaa/bbb in the figure)

It is the responsibility of the Frame Relay network to correlate a Q.933 Frame Relay address (E.164) to a DLCI at dd in the figure. Likewise, it the responsibility of the ATM network to correlate a Q.2931 ATM address to a VPI/VCI at yyy/zzz in the figure.

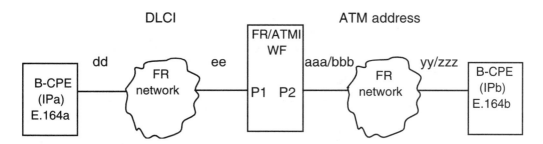

Figure 6–10   Configuration for address resolution.

ARP Message Formats

For Frame Relay-ATM interworking, ARP is modified as shown in Figure 6–11 with the notes depicted in Table 6–3.

The ATM Forum defines three structures for the combined use of number and subaddress:

	ATM Number	ATM Subaddress
Structure 1	ATM Forum NSAPA	null
Structure 2	E.164	null
Structure 3	E.164	ATM Forum NSAPA

TRAFFIC MANAGEMENT

The traffic management operations for Frame Relay-ATM service interworking are established in Q.933 Annex A, T1.617 Annex D and vendor-specific operations. This section focuses on the service interworking operations implemented by Nortel in its Passport and Magellan products.[1]

Traffic management across the FR-ATM IWF focuses on two areas:

1. QOS class mapping between Frame Relay and ATM, to determine emission priority and discard priority
2. Traffic management

---

[1]I thank Nortel for their information on this aspect of ATM internetworking. Further information is available in Nortel's various user and programming guides on Nortel's Magellan ATM family.

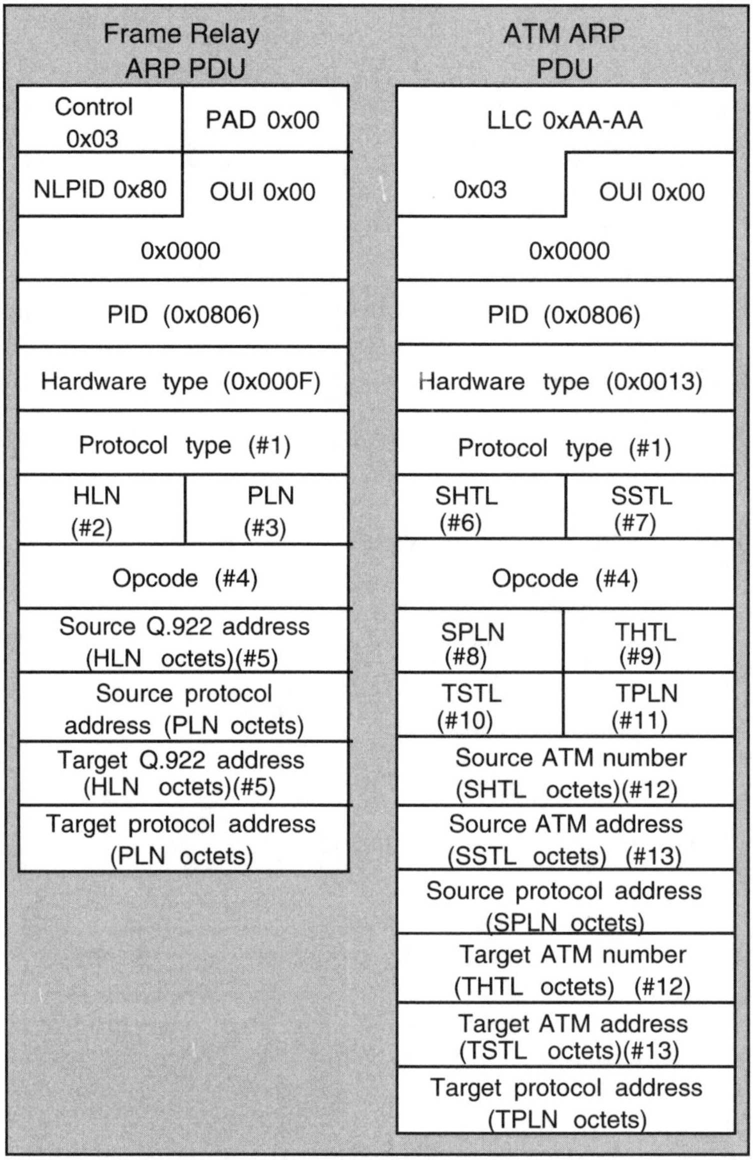

Frame Relay ARP PDU		ATM ARP PDU	
Control 0x03	PAD 0x00	LLC 0xAA-AA	
NLPID 0x80	OUI 0x00	0x03	OUI 0x00
0x0000		0x0000	
PID (0x0806)		PID (0x0806)	
Hardware type (0x000F)		Hardware type (0x0013)	
Protocol type (#1)		Protocol type (#1)	
HLN (#2)	PLN (#3)	SHTL (#6)	SSTL (#7)
Opcode (#4)		Opcode (#4)	
Source Q.922 address (HLN octets)(#5)		SPLN (#8)	THTL (#9)
Source protocol address (PLN octets)		TSTL (#10)	TPLN (#11)
Target Q.922 address (HLN octets)(#5)		Source ATM number (SHTL octets)(#12)	
Target protocol address (PLN octets)		Source ATM address (SSTL octets) (#13)	
		Source protocol address (SPLN octets)	
		Target ATM number (THTL octets) (#12)	
		Target ATM address (TSTL octets)(#13)	
		Target protocol address (TPLN octets)	

See Table 6–3 for note references #1 through #14.

Figure 6–11   ARP message PDU formats.

Table 6–3   Notes to Figure 6–11

#1: Ethertype; IP is 0x08-00

#2: HLN: Hardware address length: 2 or 4 for Frame Relay

#3: PLN: Protocol address length: 4 for IP

#4: ARP request is 1, ARP reply is 2; reverse ARP request is 3, reverse ARP reply is 4; inverse ARP request is 8, inverse ARP reply is 9; ARP NAK (ATM only) is 10

#5: C/R, FECN, BECN, and DE bits are set to zero

#6: SHTL: Type and length of source ATM number (#14)

#7: SSTL: Type and length of source ATM subaddress (#14)

#8: SPLN: Length of source protocol address: 4 for IP

#9: THTL: Type and length of target ATM number (#14)

#10: TSTL: Type and length of target ATM subaddress (#14)

#11: TPLN: Length of target protocol address: 4 for IP

#12: ATM number (E.164 or ATM Forum NSAPA)

#13: ATM subaddress (ATM Forum NSAPA)

#14: The encoding of the 8-bit type and length value for SHTL, SSTL, THTL, and TSTL is shown in Box 6–1

Box 6–1 8-Bit TLV Encoding

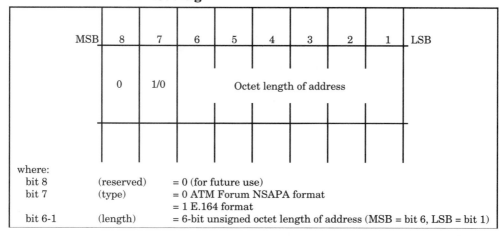

MSB	8	7	6	5	4	3	2	1	LSB
	0	1/0	Octet length of address						

where:
bit 8   (reserved)   = 0 (for future use)
bit 7   (type)   = 0 ATM Forum NSAPA format
                           = 1 E.164 format
bit 6-1   (length)   = 6-bit unsigned octet length of address (MSB = bit 6, LSB = bit 1)

Table 6–4   Emission and Discard Priorities

FR Emission Priority	Traffic Type
Class 0	Multimedia (e.g., voice) with high emission priority
Class 1	Data with medium-high emission priority
Class 2	Data with medium emission priority
Class 3	Data with normal emission priority

FR Discard Priority	Traffic Type
Class 0[1]	Control traffic (not used by Frame Relay)
Class 1	High importance
Class 2	Medium importance
Class 3[3]	Low importance

Notes
1. Not provisionable
2. Not provisionable; automatically assigned for DE = 1 traffic

Frame Relay Quality of Service

Provisioning the QOS class for a FR-ATM connection is identical to that for a FR UNI or FR NNI connection. The emission priorities and discard priorities of the connection are separately provisioned to provide the QOS desired. These priorities are summarized in Table 6–4.

ATM Quality of Service

For ATM connections, there is no change in the provisioning of a QOS class. The QOS classes are specified directly based on the traffic type, as shown in Table 6–5. The emission and discard priorities are then automatically assigned. This table is only applicable for CLP=0 traffic; CLP=1 cells are treated as having a Class 3 discard priority.

FR-ATM Quality of Service

To provide maximum versatility, and recognizing that the selection of the mapping between the Frame Relay and ATM classes of service is dependent on network traffic types and engineering considerations, no

Table 6–5 ATM QOS Classes

ATM QOS Class	QOS Class Name and Usage	Emission Priority	Discard Priority
Class 1	Constant bit rate (CBR)—ATM Forum Class A. Intended for circuit emulation and CBR video	Class 0	Class 1
Class 2	Variable bit rate (VBR) Real Time—ATM Forum Class B. Intended for packetized audio and VBR video	Class 1	Class 1
Class 3	Connection oriented (CO)—ATM Forum Class C. Intended for connection-oriented protocols	Class 2	Class 2
Class 4	Connectionless (CNLS)—ATM Forum Class D. Intended for connectionless protocols	Class 2	Class 2
Class 0	Unspecified bit rate (UBR)	Class 2	Class 3

restrictions are imposed on the selection of the available QOS classes. The network provider can tailor this mapping to best match network capacity.

Table 6–6 shows a typical mapping between the Frame Relay and ATM QOS classes. Voice applications are assigned to the highest Frame Relay emission priority and the ATM VBR class. This table also differentiates between three types of data. This differentiation allows the best match of application demands to network performance.

The discard priority of the connection is also dependent on the settings of the Frame Relay DE and ATM CLP bits. Based on the assump-

Table 6–6 FR-ATM Typical Mapping between FR and ATM QOS Classes

Traffic Type	FR Emission Priority	FR Discard Priority	ATM QOS Class	ATM QOS Name
Packetized Voice	Class 0	Class 1	Class 2	VBR
Data	Class 1	Class 2	Class 2/3	VBR/CO
Data	Class 2	Class 2	Class 3	CO/CNLS
Data	Class 3	Class 3	Class 0	UBR

Note: Frame Relay discard priority Class 3 is not directly provisionable. Traffic can be forced to DE = 1 by provisioning CIR = 0.

Table 6–7 Discard Priority Mapping

ATM CLP	Provisioned Frame Relay Discard Priority	Resulting FR Discard Priority	Frame Relay DE
0	Class 1	Class 1	0
0	Class 2	Class 2	0
1	Don't care	Class 3	1

Frame Relay DE	ATM Discard Priority (see Note)	Resulting ATM Discard Priority	ATM CLP
0	Class 1	Class 1	0
0	Class 2	Class 2	0
0	Class 3	Class 3	1
1	Don't care	Class 3	1

Note: Provisioned by selecting ATM QOS.

tion that the DE-CLP mapping option is enabled, Table 6–7 shows the effect that these bits have on the connection discard priority that results from applying FR-ATM IWF for each direction.

Connection Policing and Traffic Shaping

A typical strategy is to perform policing at the receiving interface on the network and traffic shaping at the ATM transmit interface (if connected to an external ATM network). This strategy protects the network from excessive traffic on particular connections and offers some buffering to smooth out the inherent bursts that results from frame-to-cell conversion.

Standard Frame Relay rate enforcement of committed information rate (CIR) and excess information rate (EIR) with tagging applies. Applicable provisionable parameters at the Frame Relay ingress are CIR, Bc, and Be. The typical ATM traffic parameters are PCR_{0+1}, SCR_0, and the MBS. These parameters are specified at every ATM hop as well as at the ATM endpoint where shaping is enabled.

The mapping between these traffic parameters is subject to engineering considerations, and is largely dependent on the balance between acceptable loss probabilities and network costs.

SUMMARY

Chapter 6 has explained how service interworking relieves the ATM user from the need to know about the remote Frame Relay system and vice versa. Note that the Frame Relay and ATM user perform no mapping services because the IWF is responsible for the mapping services, and that service interworking defines a wide variety of encapsulation and header mapping functions.

7

Introduction to LAN Emulation

T his chapter introduces ATM LAN Emulation (LANE). A review is made of the major operations of LANs in relation to ATM, and the rationale for the use of LANE is examined. A description is provided of the major LANE components, which consists of a variety of clients and servers.

Once again, we examine the Address Resolution Protocol (ARP) and learn how the LANE version of ARP is used to resolve MAC and ATM addresses. The chapter introduces LANE virtual channel connections (VCCs) and compares control and data virtual channels. The chapter also describes the LANE interfaces (SAPs and service definitions) between the layers of the LANE model.[1]

The chapter concludes with a description of the role of Q.2931 in the setting up of VCCs.

COMPARING LANS AND ATM

Much of the traffic sent between user equipment emanates and terminates over local area networks (LANs), the most prominent being Ethernet/IEEE 802.3, and IEEE 802.5 networks.

---

[1]The terms service specifications and service definitions are used interchangeably in this book.

As discussed in Chapter 1, LAN traffic is considerably different from ATM traffic because LAN traffic is connectionless and ATM traffic is connection-oriented. Moreover, since LANs use a shared medium, it is an easy matter to provide multicast and broadcast operations. Certainly, multicast and broadcast features can be provided in an ATM network, but these services require more operations on the part of the ATM switch than in a simpler LAN configuration. The ATM switch must use a routing table to determine which output port the traffic is to be sent to.

LAN addresses, which identify a LAN user workstation, are based on the well-known MAC address. This address is a serial number of the manufacturer of the LAN card and another number chosen by the LAN manufacturer. These flat, non-hierarchical addresses have nothing to do with the identification of the network and are therefore independent of a network topology. ATM addresses are based on the OSI addressing conventions and can identify networks, subnetworks, hosts, and other entities.

Purpose of LAN Emulation (LANE)

If an enterprise wishes to migrate to ATM technology, it is faced with the fact that ATM and LAN technologies are quite different. It is best not to change any components on an end user station during the migration to and installation of ATM networks. LAN emulation is designed to provide transparency to the end user application and permits the applications to interact with each other as if ATM did not exist. Table 7–1 provides a summary of these concepts.

The LAN emulation specification published by the ATM Forum is based on emulating the LAN MAC service. It does not explore operations at the network layer, which is left to other specifications, covered in Chapters 10 and 11 of this book.

Table 7–1   LAN Emulation (LANE)

- ATM and LAN technologies are different.
- User equipment should not be changed during migration to ATM networks.
- LAN emulation is designed to provide transparency to the end user application.
- LAN emulation permits users to interact with each other as if ATM did not exist.
- The LAN emulation specification (published by the ATM Forum) is based on emulating the LAN MAC service.
- LAN emulation does not explore the emulation of the network layer, which is left to other specifications.

SUPPORT OF KEY LAN OPERATIONS

The ATM Forum LAN emulation specification is designed to support several key LAN operations. First, connectionless operations are emulated. This operation means that the LAN stations can function as usual and need not be concerned with setting up connections before sending traffic. Even though the traffic traverses across ATM connections, end users are not aware of the connection-oriented part of the transfer process. LAN emulation supports MAC broadcast or multicast operations. LAN emulation supports MAC driver interfaces in ATM stations. This concept allows existing applications to access an ATM network through traditional protocol stacks such as IP, IPX, APPN, and AppleTalk. In today's environment, these protocol stacks operate directly over the MAC layer with a MAC driver. Therefore, LAN emulation must offer the same MAC driver service primitives to the upper layers so that they do not have to change their interface to the MAC layer.

Several "standardized" interfaces are available for MAC device drivers. The Network Driver Device Specification (NDIS) is available from 3COM/Microsoft under the *LAN Manager: Network Driver Interface Specification*, October 8, 1990. The Open Data Link Interface (ODI) is available from Novell, Inc. under the *Open Data Link Interface Developers Guide,* March 20, 1992. The Data Link Provider Interface (DLPI) is available from UNIX, International under *Data Link Provider Interface (DLPI) Specification,* Revision 2.0.0, OSI Workgroup, August 1991.

LAN EMULATION COMPONENTS

Thus far in the development of LANE, each emulated LAN is either an Ethernet/IEEE 802.3 or IEEE 802.5 network. Regardless of the specific LAN, each emulated LAN must consist of the following entities (see Figure 7–1):

- A set of LAN emulation clients (LE clients or LECs)
- A single LAN emulation service (LE service)
  The LE service consists of the following:
  - An LE configuration server (LECS)
  - An LE server (LES)
  - A broadcast and unknown server (BUS)

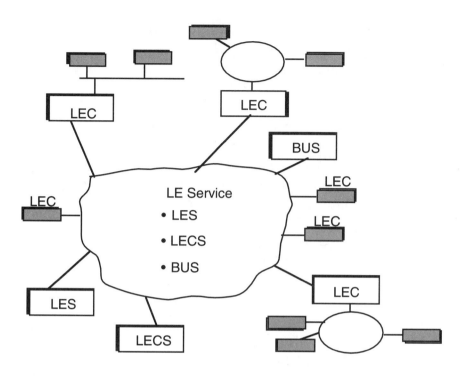

where:
  BUS   Broadcast and Unknown Server
  LEC   AN Emulation Client
  LECS   LAN Emulation Configuration Server
  LES   LAN Emulation Server

Figure 7–1   LAN Emulation components.

The LE client is housed within an ATM end station. The LE client represents a set of users, which are identified by their MAC addresses. In contrast, the LE service may be part of an end station or may be housed in a switch. Moreover, it may be centralized into one station or distributed over multiple stations.

The major functions and attributes of these entities are as follows:

1. LEC
   • Entity in end system that sends data and performs address resolution
   • Bridges LAN frames between LANs (using MAC addresses)[2]

---

[2]A component that connects these conventional (legacy) LANs and an ATM network is also called an edge device. This component is examined in more detail in Chapter 11.

- Contains ATM interfaces for emulated LAN
- Identified by an ATM address
- Associated with MAC stations (MAC addresses), reachable through its ATM address

2. LES
   - Used to register MAC addresses, resolve MAC/ATM addresses (802.5 route descriptors)
   - Responds to LEC address resolution requests
   - Identified by an ATM address
   - Configured as one LES per emulated LAN

3. BUS
   - Acts as a multicast server by handling data sent by LEC with MAC addresses of "all 1s"
   - Each LEC is associated with one BUS
   - Handles unknown destination traffic (before a target ATM address has been resolved)
   - May be multiple BUSs per ELAN
   - Identified by an ATM address

4. LECS
   - Assigns LE clients to emulated LANs
   - . . . does so by giving the LEC the ATM address of the LES and a number of operating parameters (discussed later)
   - One LECS serves all ELANs, if multiple ELANs exist within a system

The location of these entities is not defined. For efficiency of operations, they should be housed in routers or ATM switches.

REGISTRATIONS

Figure 7–2 shows how a LAN emulation client makes known its ATM address and the MAC addresses for which it is responsible. Using the registration procedure, LEC A provides the LES its ATM addresses and the MAC addresses of the workstation (WS) on its attached LANs.[3] Thereafter, when other entities need to know about these address bindings, they can send queries to the LES.

---

[3]The specific configuration might have the LEC operating in a bridge. Alternately, a bridge could be located behind a separate node that houses the LEC.

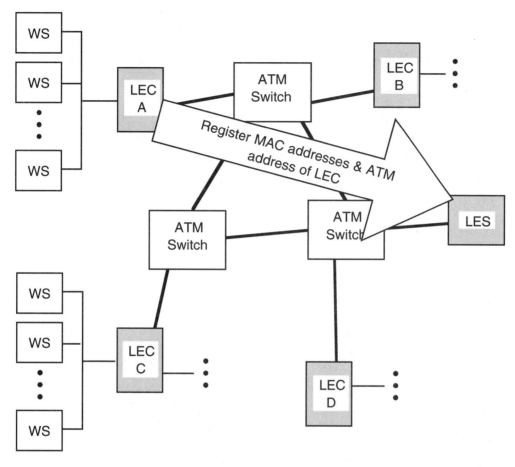

where: WS = Workstation

Figure 7–2   The registration operation.

ARP OPERATIONS

In Figure 7–3, LEC C receives a LAN frame with the MAC destination address of A in the frame header. Since LEC C does not know the ATM address associated with MAC address A, it sends a query to its LES. This query takes the form of an ARP request message.

Because LEC A had previously registered MAC address A and ATM address 123 with the LES that is servicing LEC C, it is an easy matter for the LES to inform LEC C about the queried address binding. This operation is performed with the ARP response message (see Figure 7–4).

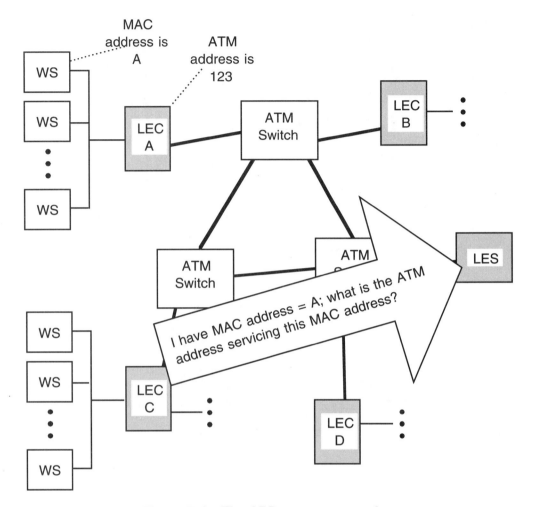

Figure 7–3   The ARP request operation.

CONNECTION SETUP

Now that LEC C knows where to reach MAC address A, it can set up an ATM connection to the LEC responsible for this MAC address. As shown in Figure 7–5, this process entails a setup operation with a switched virtual call (SVC). Later discussions will explain this call setup operation in more detail.

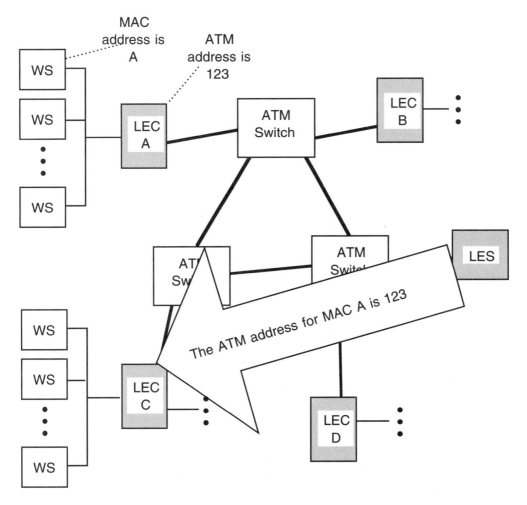

Figure 7–4   The ARP response operation.

VIRTUAL CHANNELS

As shown in Figure 7–6, communication among LE clients and between LE clients and the LE service occurs through ATM virtual channel connections (VCCs). Control and data VCCs are established for LAN emulation and each LE client must communicate with the LE service over these VCCs. The technology supports switched virtual circuits (SVCs), or permanent virtual circuits (PVCs).

As shown in Figure 7–6b, LAN emulation consists of a user-to-network interface (UNI), which is called LAN Emulation UNI, or LUNI.

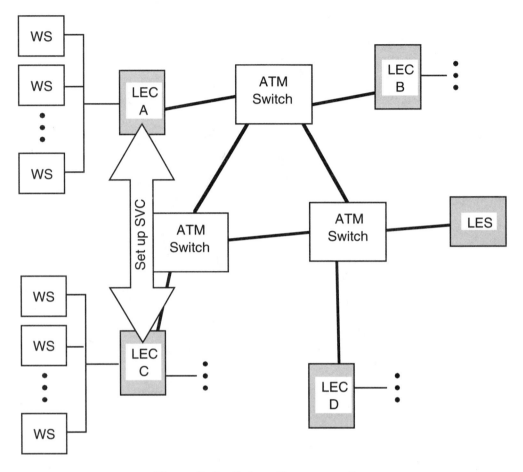

Figure 7–5   Set up the connection.

The LUNI specifies the protocol interactions between an LE client and the LE service over the ATM network.

LANE USE OF PRIMITIVES (SERVICE DEFINITIONS)

It is worthwhile to review the concepts of service primitives (also called service definitions and introduced in Chapter 2) as they pertain to layer interactions and their relationship to the protocols that flow across the UNI. The primitive is used by the layer to invoke the service entities and create any headers that will be used by the peer layer in the remote station. This point is quite important. The primitives are received by ad-

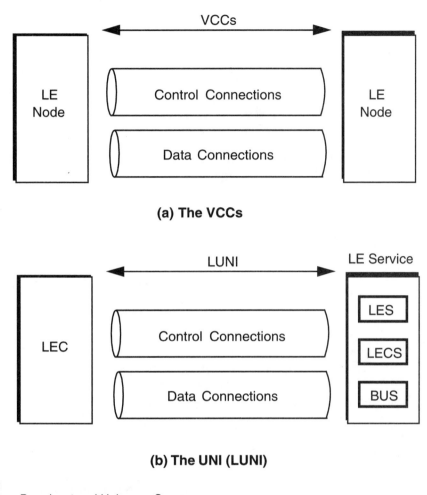

(a) The VCCs

(b) The UNI (LUNI)

where:
BUS   Broadcast and Unknown Server
LEC   LAN Emulation Client
LECS   LAN Emulation Configuration Server
LES   LAN Emulation Server

Figure 7–6   Virtual channel connections (VCCs) and the UNI.

jacent layers in the local site and are used to create the headers used by peer layers at the remote site.

At the receiving site, the primitive is used to convey the data to the next and adjacent upper layer and to inform this layer about the actions of the lower layer. These concepts are shown in a general way in Figure 7–7. For LAN emulation, primitives are defined between the LAN emulation entity (layer) and upper layer protocols (ULPs, also called the ser-

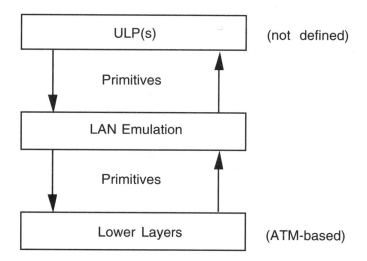

Figure 7–7   Primitives.

vice user). These upper layers are not defined in the LAN emulation specifications. Primitives are also defined between LAN emulation and lower layers, which we shall see are ATM-based layers. Chapter 8 provides a detailed description of these operations.

THE LANE PROTOCOL MODEL

Figure 7–8 shows the LAN Emulation layered model. As the reader can see, the LAN Emulation entity (layer) makes use of ATM layers and sublayers.

The layer interactions occur through four sets of service definitions labeled 1 through 4 in Figure 7–8. The service definitions are examined later in Chapter 8, but for our initial discussions, a brief summary is provided of each of the service definition interfaces:

- *Interface 1:* This interface defines the interactions with service definitions between the LAN emulation layer and upper layers, principally for the transmitting and receiving of user traffic. Since the on-going user layers are not to be affected with the ELAN operations. This interface is where the NDIS and ODI interfaces come into play.

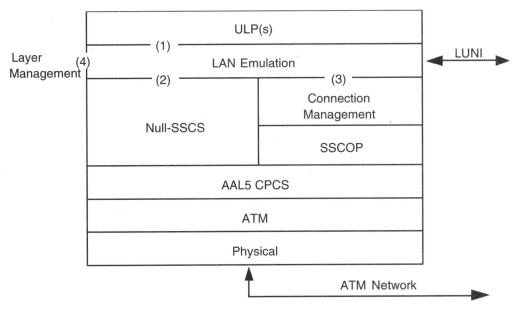

where:
    AAL   ATM adaptation layer
    ATM   Asynchronous transfer mode
    CPCS   Common part convergence sublayer
    LAN   Local area network
    SSCOP   Service specific connection-oriented protocol
    SSCS   Service specific convergence sublayer
    ULP   Upper layer protocol(s)

Figure 7–8   LANE layered model.

- *Interface 2:* This interface defines the interactions with service definitions between the LAN emulation layer and the ATM adaptation layer (AAL), principally for the sending and receiving of AAL5 protocol data units (PDUs). Keep in mind (from previous chapters) that AAL5 accesses lower layers, including the ATM and physical layers. The interface service access points (SAPs) are identified by SAP-IDs. These SAP-IDs have a one-to-one mapping to VCCs.

- *Interface 3:* This interface defines the interactions with service definitions between the LAN emulation layer and the connection management entity. These service definitions are used to set up and release VCCs. Remember that this entity must handle both SVCs and PVCs.

- *Interface 4:* This interface defines the interactions with service definitions between the LAN emulation layer and the layer management entity. Its purpose is to initialize and control the LAN emulation entity and to receive status information about the ongoing LAN emulation operations.

PRINCIPAL LUNI FUNCTIONS

Figure 7–9 provides a functional view of the LAN emulation user-to-network interface (LUNI). Notice that the interface defines the operations between the LAN emulation clients (LECS, which are housed in an ATM end system) and the LAN emulation service. The requirements for the LUNI pertain to (1) initialization, (2) registration, (3) address resolution, and (4) data transfer.

The initialization operation entails obtaining the ATM addresses of the LE service, joining or leaving an emulated LAN (which is specified by the ATM address of the LE service), and declaring if a particular LE client wishes to receive address resolution requests for any traffic with unregistered destinations.

The registration operation entails the furnishing of a list of individual MAC addresses (and/or a list of Token Ring source-route descriptors) that the LE client represents. These source-routed descriptors consist of 802.5 segment/bridge pairs that are used for source-route bridging.

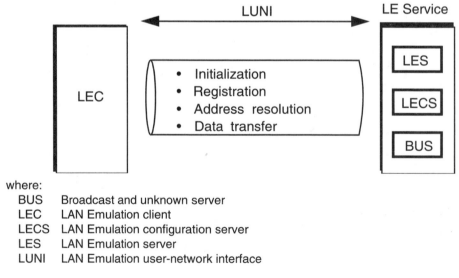

where:
  BUS   Broadcast and unknown server
  LEC   LAN Emulation client
  LECS   LAN Emulation configuration server
  LES   LAN Emulation server
  LUNI   LAN Emulation user-network interface

Figure 7–9   LUNI functions.

The address resolution operation is used to obtain the ATM address(es) (that represents the LE client) with a particular MAC address. This MAC address may take the form of a unicast address, a broadcast address, or a segment pair.

The data transfer operation moves traffic from the source to destination by encapsulating the LE service data unit (LE-SDU) into an AAL5 PDU for transmission by the LE client. It also entails the forwarding of the AAL5 PDU by the LE service, and the receiving and decapsulating of the AAL5 frame by the LE client.

CONTROL AND DATA CHANNEL CONNECTION

Control Channel Connections

We have learned that LAN emulation operations take place over virtual channel connections (VCCs). The connections are organized around control connections and data connections. The control connections are used for control traffic such as address resolution requests and responses. The data VCCs are used to transmit encapsulated LAN frames. Each VCC carries traffic for one emulated LAN, and the VCCs are provisioned to support a mesh of connections between the LAN emulation entities.

Let us examine the control connections first. The control VCC links the following entities: LEC to LECS and LEC to LES. They are never allowed to carry user traffic and they are set up as part of the LEC initialization phase, which is discussed later in this chapter.

Currently, three control connections are defined in the specification (see Figure 7–10): (1) configuration direct VCC, (2) control direct VCC, and (3) control distribute VCC.

The configuration direct VCC is used to obtain configuration information and may be setup by the LEC (as an option) as part of the LECS connect operation. The entity is allowed to maintain the configuration direct VCC while participating in the emulated LAN. That is to say, it can keep this connection open for further queries to the LE configuration service while participating in the overall emulated LAN operations. This channel can also be used to inquire about other LE clients (by other, I mean other than the one to which the channel is attached). As we shall see later, this connection uses broadband low layer information (B-LLI) to indicate that it is carrying LE control traffic.

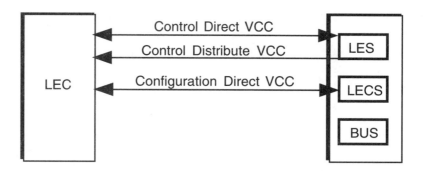

where:
  BUS   Broadcast and unknown server
  LEC   LAN Emulation client
  LECS   LAN Emulation configuration server
  LES   LAN Emulation server

Figure 7–10   Control channel.

The second control connection is the control direct VCC. It operates between the LEC and the LES in a bidirectional manner for sending ongoing control traffic. It is set up by the LEC during the initialization phase and, since it is bidirectional, it implies that the LEC must accept control traffic from this connection. This connection must be maintained by the LEC and the LES while these entities participate in the emulated LAN.

The last control connection is the control distribute VCC. This VCC is typically set up by the LES during the initialization phase. The use of this connection is optional and, if implemented, is set up in unidirectional point-to-point or point-to-multipoint arrangement. It is used by the LEC to distribute control traffic to the LEC or LECS. If this channel is established, the LEC is required to accept the traffic on the channel. And finally, both the LEC and LES must keep this connection up while participating in the emulated LAN.

Data Channel Connections

The data connections are used to send traffic between the LECs, which as we learned earlier are Ethernet/IEEE 802.3 or IEEE 802.5 frames. The data connections can also support flush messages, which are explained in more detail later. The flush message is a control message, but this is the only control traffic the data VCCs can support.

Currently, three data connections are defined in the specification (see Figure 7–11): (1) data direct VCC, (2) multicast send VCC, and (3) multicast forward VCC.

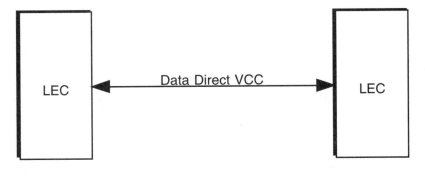

(a) Data direct VCC

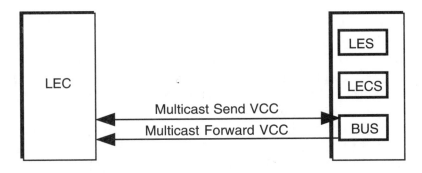

(b) Multicast send VCC and multicast forward VCC

where:
  BUS   Broadcast and unknown server
  LEC   LAN Emulation client
  LECS   LAN Emulation configuration server
  LES   LAN Emulation server

Figure 7–11   Data channel connections

The data direct VCC is used to transmit unicast traffic between LECS. Let us assume an LE client has traffic to send but it does not know the relevant ATM address for the destination node. The LE client generates an address resolution request to learn about the ATM address for the destination. The address resolution request, based on ARP, is called the LE_ARP message. Upon receiving a reply to the LE_ARP request, it can then establish a data direct VCC. Thereafter, all traffic can be sent to the destination LAN. The LEC that initiates the LE_ARP operations is responsible for establishing the data direct VCC with the responding client that was identified in the LE_ARP response. If the data direct VCC cannot be established (for example, due to bandwidth limitations), the LEC is not allowed to send traffic to the BUS. Its only option is to disconnect an existing data direct VCC in order to free up resources.

The second type of data connections is the multicast send VCC. This channel is setup with the BUS. It uses the same procedures that we discussed for data direct VCCs (using LE_ARP). The multicast send VCC allows the LEC to send multicast traffic to the BUS and to send initial unicast traffic to the BUS. In turn, the BUS uses the VCC return path to send traffic to the LEC. And, once again, this VCC must be maintained by the LEC while it participates in the emulated LAN.

The last data connection is the multicast forward VCC. It is utilized after the LEC has established the multicast send VCC. This VCC is used by the BUS to send traffic to the LEC. The multicast forward VCC can be either point-to-multipoint or unidirectional point-to-point. An important rule associated with this channel is that it must be established from the BUS to the LEC before the LEC can participate in the emulated LAN and, as in the other channels, the LEC should maintain this VCC while participating in the emulated LAN.

Another rule should be stated at this point. The BUS is allowed to forward traffic to the LEC on the multicast send VCC or the multicast forward VCC. However, the BUS is not allowed to send duplicate traffic on these two channels. But the LEC must accept traffic from each of them.

THE INITIALIZATION FUNCTION

The functions of the LAN emulation service are organized around (1) initialization, (2) registration, (3) address resolution, (4) connection management, and (5) data transfer.

This section will explain the initialization function with reference to Figure 7–12. As the figure illustrates, the initialization function proceeds from an initial state to an operational state through five phases.

In the initial state, the LE server and LE clients have parameters stored dealing with addresses, operational characteristics, and so on, which are discussed later. This information is about themselves that they will eventually share with other entities.

The first phase in the initialization function is called the LECS connect phase and entails the LE client finding and establishing a configura-

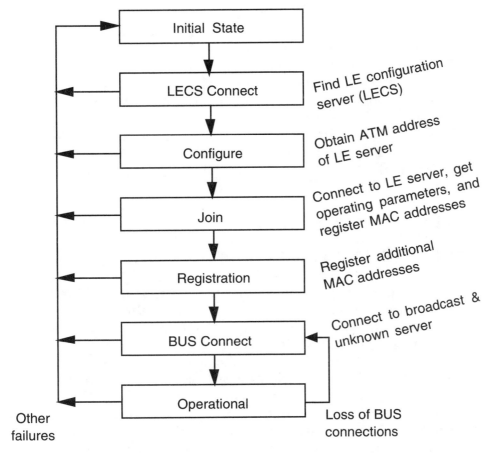

Figure 7–12 The initialization function.

tion direct VCC to the LE configuration server. The LECS is located through a predetermined procedure: (a) an ILMI (Interim Local Management Interface) operation or (b) an established PVC (permanent virtual circuit) to the LECS.

The next phase is the configuration phase in which the LE client discovers the LE service, which entails obtaining the ATM address of the clients' LE server. Also, during this phase, the LECs will downline load several operating parameters to the client. During this phase, the characteristics of the emulated LAN are given by the LEC to the LECS (type of LAN, maximum frame size).

Next, in the join phase, the LE client sets up a control direct VCC to the LE server. Upon completion of the join phase, the LE client will be identified with a unique LE client identifier (LECID). In addition, the LES now knows the emulated LAN's type (i.e., Ethernet), and the emulated LAN's maximum frame size, and the LEC has registered its MAC and ATM addresses with the LES.

The next phase is called registration. This operation allows the LE client to register one or more than one MAC addresses, and/or route descriptors with the LE server.

The final phase is the bus connect phase, which requires that the LE client send LE_ARPs for the all 1s broadcast MAC address. Once this is received by the BUS, it can then set up the multicast forward VCC to the LE client.

ADDRESS RESOLUTION OPERATIONS

As just explained, the registration procedure is used for a client to provide address information to the LAN emulation server. Consequently, this LE server can respond to address resolution requests if the LECs have previously registered their LAN addresses.

Assuming registration operations have been performed properly, the address resolution procedure allows a LAN destination address to be associated with an ATM address of another client or the BUS itself. The purpose of the address resolution procedure is to provide a mechanism for setting up the proper data connect VCCs to carry the traffic.

Upon receiving a frame in which the destination MAC address is unknown to the LEC, this LEC issues an LE_ARP request frame to the LES on its control direct VCC (see Figure 7–13). Upon receiving this request, the LES can issue an LE_ARP reply on behalf of a client that has previously registered the requested MAC destination address with the LES, which is shown in the bottom part of Figure 7–13. Otherwise, the LES forwards this LE_ARP frame to an appropriate client or clients on the control distribute VCC or 1-to-n control direct VCCs. Assuming that a client responds to the LE_ARP request with an LE_ARP reply, the LES will relay this reply over the control distribute VCC, which is shown in the top part of Figure 7–13.

Like conventional ARP operations, an LE_ARP client maintains an LE_ARP cache that stores the information contained in the LE_ARP replies. The cache is managed through timers that "age" the cache entries. I will provide more information about LE_ARP cache later in this book.

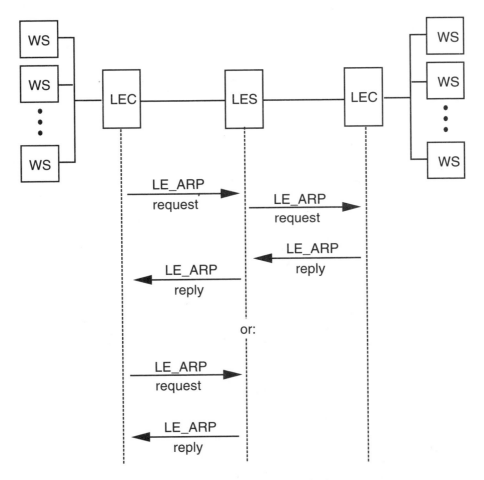

Figure 7–13   Address resolution.

CONNECTION ESTABLISHMENT PROCEDURES

In order to use the data direct VCC, a version of Q.2931 is implemented to support a call establishment. This is shown in a Figure 7–14, which deals with the protocol stack in Figure 7–8, titled "Connection Management."

Figure 7–14 shows the use of the Q.2931 SETUP, CONNECT, and CONNECT ACK messages. These messages are explained briefly in this chapter and they are covered in detail in Volume II of this series. The READY_IND and READY_QUERY are defined in the LAN emulation specification.

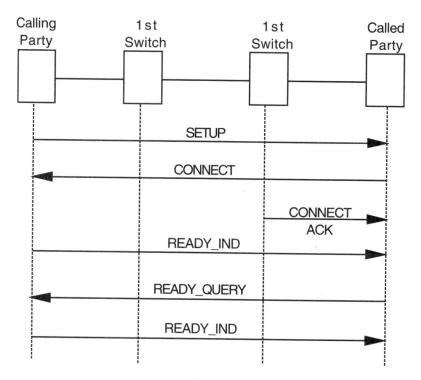

Figure 7–14   Establishment procedures.

A few rules should be clarified at this time pertaining to call establishment operations. First, the called party should not send a CONNECT message until it is ready to receive frames on the new VCC. This obviously means that the calling party assumes the VCC is available when it receives the CONNECT message. Since the CONNECT ACK message has local significance only on the called party side, the called party does not know that its initial data will be received by the calling party until it receives some end-to-end indication from the far end. This situation is endemic to the way that Q.2931 operates. In turn, upon receiving a CONNECT message, the calling party knows the allocation of the VPI/VCI values. The CONNECT message also allows the calling party to enable itself to receive traffic.

The READY_IND message is sent by the calling party after it has performed its housekeeping chores and is ready to receive frames on the VCC. It may also begin to send traffic immediately on the VCC. Upon receiving the CONNECT ACK message, the called party starts a timer. The use of this timer overcomes the problem with the local nature of the CONNECT ACK message. Upon expiration of the timer, if the called party has not received the READY_IND message, it can send a READY_QUERY message to the calling party on the VCC. In effect, this "ping" assures that both parties are aware of the connection. As Figure 7–14 shows, the calling party must respond to the READY_QUERY message with a READY_IND message.

The SETUP Message

Figure 7–15 shows the information elements associated with the SETUP message. A brief description of these information elements follow.

The AAL parameters information element contains five fields.

1. AAL type: Coded as 5 to stipulate the use of AAL5.
2. Forward maximum CPCS-SDU size: Coded to indicate the number of octets for this field; value depends on type of LAN being used.
3. Backward maximum CPCS-SDU size: Coded to indicate the number of octets for this field; value depends on the type of LAN being used.

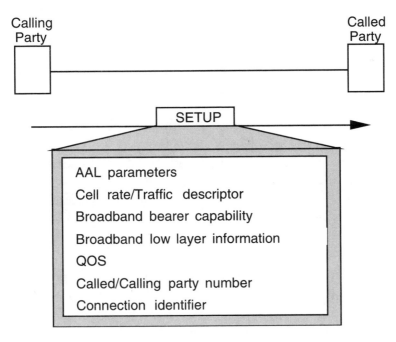

Figure 7–15   Contents of the SETUP message.

4. Mode: Coded as 1 to indicate message mode.

5. SSCS type: Coded as 0 to indicate null SSCS.

The ATM user cell rate/ATM traffic descriptor information element contains three fields.

1. Forward peak cell rate: Coded to indicate line rate in cells per second.

2. Backward peak cell rate: Coded to indicate line rate in cells per second.

3. Best effort indicator: Coded as 0xBE.

The broadband bearer capability information element contains five fields.

4. Bearer class: Coded as 16 to indicate BCOB-x.

5. Traffic type: Coded as 0 to indicate no indication.

6. Timing requirements: Coded as 0 to indicate no indication.

7. Susceptible to clipping: Coded as 0 to indicate not susceptible to clipping.

8. User plane connection configuration: Coded as 0 for point-to-point and 1 for point-to-multipoint.

The broadband low layer information element contains five fields.

- User information layer 3 protocol: Coded as 11 to identify the ISO/IEC TR9577 specification is to be used to identify an encapsulation header.

- ISO/TR 9577 Initial Protocol Identifier: Coded as 0x64 to identify a SNAP header.

- SNAP ID: Coded as 0x80 to indicate that the SNAP organization unit identifier (OUI) and the protocol identifier follow.

- SNAP organization unit identifier (OUI): Coded as 0x00-A0-3E to identify the ATM Forum OUI.

- PID: Coded with several values to indicate the type of VCC that is being setup, the rules for this field are described in Chapter 2.

The QOS information element contains two fields.

1. QOS class forward: Coded as 0 to indicate class 0.
2. QOS class backward: Coded as 0 to indicate class 0.

The called party number and calling party number information elements contain the fields pertaining to the ATM address format (discussed in Appendix B).

The last information element is the connection identifier which contains the VPI/VCI values that are assigned by the network for the connection. The called party uses these parameters to identify the VCC being established.

RULES FOR SENDING USER TRAFFIC

LAN emulation defines two types of paths for the transfer of user traffic (data frames). The first path is used between individual LAN emulation clients and is the data direct VCC described earlier. The other type of transfer uses the multicast send VCC and multicast forward VCC for the LEC-to-BUS communications process.

Assuming that the LAN emulation client knows the relationship of the MAC destination address to the ATM address, then it can simply send the traffic across the data direct VCC. However, if the client does not know which data direct VCC to use for the destination MAC address or if the data direct VCC has not been established, it is allowed to send this traffic over the multicast VCC to the broadcast and unknown server (BUS). It is then the responsibility of the BUS to forward the traffic to the destination client. If the MAC address is not registered, then the frame must be forwarded to all known clients.

Multicast operations are implemented in a slightly different manner than unicast operations. The rule is simple: for a multicast MAC address the LE client sends these frames to the BUS and not to the client. This means that during address resolution for multicast and broadcast traffic, the ATM address of the BUS is provided and not the end clients. In turn, if an LE client wishes to receive multicast traffic, it need only be connected to the BUS.

SPANNING TREE OPERATIONS

To prevent the looping of traffic, the ELAN runs the IEEE 802.1 spanning tree protocol. If a loop is detected, a node must block one of ports that is involved in the loop. Because ARP table entries may exist after a node is no longer present, a LE_TOPOLOGY_REQUEST message is used by the LEC upon encountering a bridge configuration update message. The LE_TOPOLOGY_REQUEST message is sent to the LES, which informs other LECs. This approach allows the ARP cache entry to be aged-out sooner.

SUMMARY

LAN emulation is designed to provide transparency to the end user application when interworking LANs with ATM machines. LAN emulation permits Ethernet and Token Ring users to interact with each other as if ATM did not exist.

The LAN emulation specification (published by the ATM Forum) is based on emulating the LAN MAC service. Upper layer protocol "emulation" (e.g., L_3) is not covered in LANE. MAC and ATM Forum addresses must be used in LAN Emulation.

8

Service Specifications[1]
and Protocol Data Units (PDUs)

T his chapter examines the four sets of service specifications that were introduced in the previous chapter. The chapter also describes the protocol data units (PDUs) employed in LANE.

As a brief review, service specifications are useful to designers because they provide guidance on programming the interfaces to drivers. Recall also that LAN emulation stipulates four service specifications: (1) LAN emulation-ULP, (2) LAN emulation-AAL, (3) LAN emulation-connection management, and (4) LAN emulation-layer management.

BASIC CONCEPTS

Service specifications are implemented with primitives. For the programmer, a primitive is better known as a system or function call. The primitive defines the "transaction" between the layers.

The OSI Model makes use of illustrations that show how the layers interact with each other (see Figure 8–1): The OSI Model refers to layers with the terms N, N+1, and N-1. The particular layer that is the focus of

---

[1]As a reminder, the OSI service definitions are called service specifications in LANE.

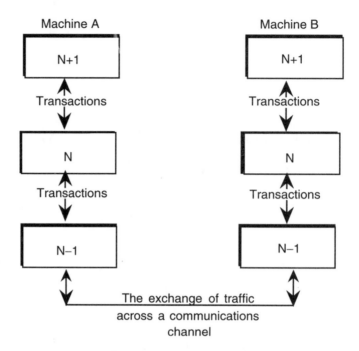

Figure 8–1   Documenting layer interactions.

attention is designated as layer N. Thereafter, the adjacent upper layer to layer N is designated as layer N+1 and the adjacent lower layer to layer N is designated as layer N–1.

In this manner, designers can use generic terms in describing the OSI layers. Moreover, the transactions between the layers can be developed in a more generic sense as well.

The services invoked at a layer are dictated by the upper layer passing primitives (transactions) to the lower layer. In Figure 8–2, users A and B communicate with each other through a lower layer.

Services are provided from the lower layer to the upper layer through a service access point (SAP). The SAP is an identifier that identifies the entity in N+1 that is performing the service(s) for layer N.

An entity in machine A can invoke some services in machine B through the use of SAPs. For example, a user that sends traffic can identify itself with a source SAP id (SSAP). It identifies the recipient of the traffic with a destination SAP value (DSAP).

It is the responsibility of the receiving lower layer N (in concert, of course, with the operating system in the receiving machine) to pass the traffic to the proper destination SAP in layer N+1. If multiple entities

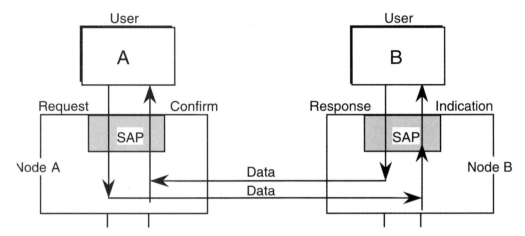

Figure 8–2   Communications between adjacent layers.

(e.g., processes) exist in the machine, the DSAP serves to properly identify the process.

The primitive is used by the layer to invoke the service entities and create any headers that will be used by the peer layer in the remote station. This point is quite important. The primitives are received by adjacent layers in the local site and are used to create the headers used by peer layers at the remote site. At the receiving site, the primitive is used to convey the data to the next and adjacent upper layer, and to inform this layer about the actions of the lower layer.

The OSI Model uses four types of primitives, summarized in Table 8–1, to perform the actions between the layers. The manner in which they are invoked varies. Not all four primitives must be invoked with each operation. For example, if the remote machine has no need to respond to the local machine, it need not return a response primitive. In this situation, a request primitive would be invoked at the local site to get the operation started. At the remote site, the indication primitive would be invoked to complete the process.

Of course, if the remote station were to send traffic back, it would invoke the operation with a response primitive, which would be mapped to the confirm primitive at the local machine.

Table 8–1   The Functions of the Service Definitions

At user A:

- *Request*. A primitive initiated by a service user to invoke a function.
- *Confirm*. A primitive response by a service provider to complete a function previously invoked by a request primitive. It may or may not follow the response primitive.

At user B:

- *Indication*. A primitive issued by a service provider to (a) invoke a function, or (b) indicate a function has been invoked.

- *Response*. A primitive response by a service user to complete a function previously invoked by an indication primitive.

LE-ULP SERVICE SPECIFICATIONS

The LE-ULP service specifications are based on the IEEE and Ethernet service specifications (see Figure 8–3). Two primitives are implemented for these service specifications. The LE_UNITDATA.request is

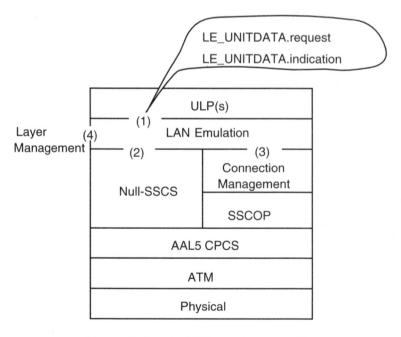

Figure 8–3   LE-ULP service specifications.

used to transfer traffic from a local entity to a remote entity and the LE_UNITDATA.indication transfers the traffic from the LAN emulation entity to the upper layer.

The parameters in the two primitives are almost identical. The only difference is that the LE_UNIDATA.indication primitive contains the service class parameter.

Each primitive contains: (1) destination address, (2) source address, (3) routing information (if applicable, for source routing on a token ring network), (4) frame type (if applicable), (5) data, and (6) priority (if applicable, for priority scheduling on a token ring network).

LE-AAL SERVICE SPECIFICATIONS

This LE-AAL service specifications defines the interface between the LAN emulation entity and AAL. As Figure 8–4 shows, the specification assumes a null SSCS. The AAL service interfaces are identified by a SAP-ID (service access point identifier) and these services apply only to the LE clients and the LE service.

Each LE client includes three types of SAPs: (1) control SAPs for initialization, registration, and address resolution; (2) data forwarding SAPs for the transfer of traffic; and (3) control SAPs that can handle configuration.

Two primitives are defined at this interface. The AAL_UNITDATA. request is used to transfer traffic from one LAN emulation layer to another. The AAL_UNITDATA.indication transfers traffic from AAL5 to the emulation layer.

Both primitives contain a SAP_ID parameter and payload parameter. The SAP_ID parameter in the request primitive is associated with the point-to-point or point-to-multipoint VCC and the payload parameter identifies the traffic that is to be transmitted. For the indication primitive, the SAP_ID is associated with the VCC on which data was received and the payload parameter identifies the received traffic.

LE-CONNECTION MANAGEMENT SERVICE SPECIFICATIONS

The LE-connection management service specifications must support permanent virtual circuits (PVCs) and switched virtual circuits (SVCs) (see Figure 8–5). The overall system must provide a mapping from a

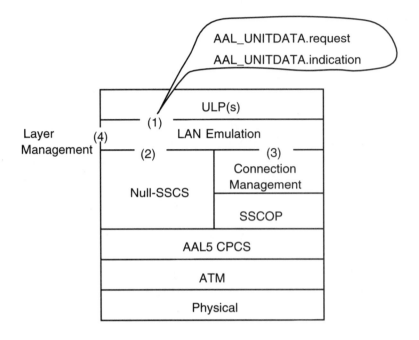

(a) The specifications

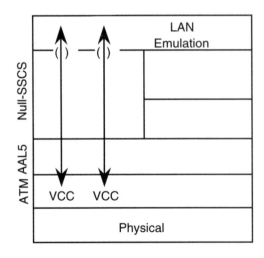

(b) SAPs and VCCs

Figure 8–4   LE-AAL service specifications.

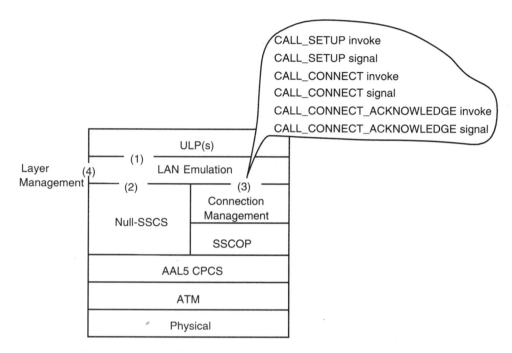

Figure 8–5   LE-connection management service specifications.

near-end ATM address, far-end ATM address, or broadband low layer information (B-LLI) to a VPI/VCI.

Since PVCs are preprovisioned, connection management is responsible for selecting an available connection that is associated with a near-end ATM address, far-end ATM address, and the B-LLI value. How these operations take place is an implementation specific matter, but the LE client must know which VPCs it is allowed to use, which PVC clients are associated with the PVCs, and which ATM addresses and B-LLI values are associated with the PVCs.

The switched virtual circuits are provided with the ATM Forum version of Q.9231. The reader may refer to Volume II of this series for more information on Q.9231. Our goal here is to explain Q.9231 in relation to LAN emulation.

First, the setup procedure is used to initiate a connection. It consists of six service specifications listed as follows:

CALL_SETUP invoke
CALL_SETUP signal
CALL_CONNECT invoke

CALL_CONNECT signal

CALL_CONNECT_ACKNOWLEDGE invoke

CALL_CONNECT_ACKNOWLEDGE signal

Parameters for the Connection Service

Table 8–2 lists the parameters that are required for a switched virtual circuit operation with LAN emulation. Once again, these parameters are defined in other standards and references. I will describe them in the context of LAN emulation. The AAL parameters defines AAL type 5 for use. The forward and backward maximum CPCS_SDU size is 1516 octets for all control VCCs and one of several options for data VCCs, as shown in Table 8–2.

Tables 8–3 and 8–4 provide more information on the LANE Q.2931 message parameters. In addition, the mode setting must equal message mode and the SSCS type must equal null SSCS.

The cell rate descriptor parameter must be coded to define both forward and backward peak cell rate in cells/second and the best effort indicator must be coded as 0xBE.

The broadband bearer capability parameter indicates what type of connection is required. The LAN emulation specification recommends using service type X or service type C as an alternative. In addition, the bearer class is set to 16, traffic type is set to 0 (no indication), timing requirements is set to 0 (no indication), susceptibility to clipping is set to 0 (not susceptive to clipping), and user plane connection configuration is set to 0 for point-to-point and 1 for point-to-multipoint.

The QOS parameter must be coded as class 0 for both forward and backward parts of the connection, which indicates a best effort requested connection.

Table 8–2   Parameters for Switched Virtual Circuit

AAL-5 SDU Max Octets	AAL-5 PDU Max Octets	Basis for SDU Size
1516	1536 (32 cells)	IEEE 802.3/Ethernet
4544	4560 (95 cells)	IEEE 802.5 Token ring 4 Mbit/s
9234	9264 (193 cells)	RFC 1628
18190	18240 (380 cells)	IEEE 802/5 token ring 16 Mbit/s

Table 8–3   Q.2931 Message Parameters Required by LAN Emulation

- AAL parameters
- ATM user cell rate/traffic descriptor
- Broadband bearer capabilities
- Broadband low layer information
- QOS parameter
- Called party number
- Calling party number
- Connection identifier

The called and calling party numbers are coded in accordance with ATM Forum address rules and must use the ATM Forum private UNI address format of 20 octets.

Finally, the connection identifier is coded to indicate what VPI, VCI values have been assigned by the network for the connection. This information is placed in the SETUP message by the network and conveyed to the called party. In turn, the VPI, VCI values are placed in this parameter in the CONNECT message and are used by the called party.

Table 8–4   The Broadband Low Layer Information Codes

Field	Value
User information layer 3 protocol	11 (ISO/IEC TR 9577)
ISO/IEC TR 9577 Initial Protocol Identifier	65 (SNAP Identifier-0x80, spread over 2 octets, left justified)
Continued from previous octet	Continued (Ext bit is set to 1)
SNAP ID	0x80 (indicates SNAP and PID follow)
SNAP Organization Unit Identifier	0x-00-A0-3E (ATM Forum OUI)
PID	0001 for LE configuration direct VCC, Control Direct VCC and Control Distribute VCC 0002 for Ethernet/IEEE 802.3 LE Data Direct VCC 0003 for IEEE 802.5 LE Data Direct VCC 0004 for Ethernet/IEEE 802.3 LE Multicast Send VCC and Multicast Forward VCC 0005 for IEEE 802.5 Multicast Send VCC and Multicast Forward VCC

Next, the release procedure is used to release a connection. It consists of four service specifications listed as follows:

CALL_RELEASE invoke
CALL_RELEASE signal
CALL_RELEASE_COMPLETE invoke
CALL_RELEASE_COMPLETE signal

ADD AND DROP PARTY PROCEDURE

The add party/drop party procedure is used to add or drop a party to an existing connection. It consists of ten service specifications listed as follows (see Figure 8–6). These operations are covered in Volume II of this series:

CALL_ADD_PARTY invoke
CALL_ADD_PARTY signal
CALL_ADD_PARTY_ACKNOWLEDGE invoke
CALL_ADD_PARTY_ACKNOWLEDGE signal
CALL_ADD_PARTY_REJECT invoke
CALL_ADD_PARTY_REJECT signal
CALL_DROP_PARTY invoke
CALL_DROP_PARTY signal
CALL_DROP_PARTY_ACKNOWLEDGE invoke
CALL_DROP_PARTY_ACKNOWLEDGE signal

LE-LAYER MANAGEMENT SERVICE SPECIFICATIONS

The LE-layer management service specifications define seven primitives at this interface. The primitives are listed in Figure 8–7 and in this section we will learn about their operations. The LM_LEC_INITIALIZE. request configures the LE client and enables it to join the emulated LAN. It is generated by the local management entity and, when received by the LE client, the client must release all VCCs, start all over again (in essence) by entering the initial state described in the previous chapter. The primitive is coded as follows:

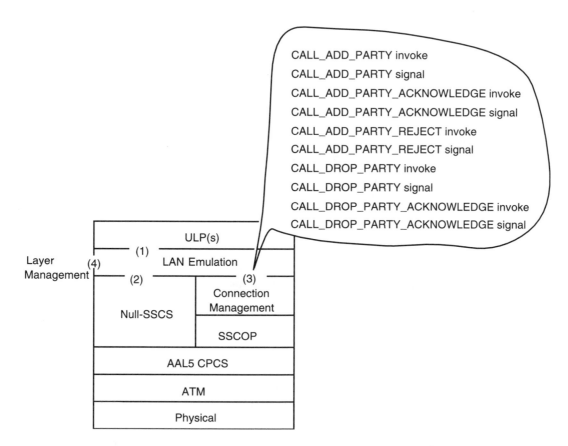

Figure 8–6 Add party/drop party service specifications.

LM_LEC_INITIALIZE.request(LEC_ATM_address, Server_ATM_address, MAC Address, Configure_mode, LEC_proxy_class, Requested_LAN_type, Requested_max_frame_size, Requested_ELAN_name, Joint_time-out)

The ATM address of the LE client is specified in LEC_ATM_address parameter. The ATM address of the LE configuration server or the LE server is contained in the Server_ATM_address parameter. The contents of this parameter depend on how the Configure_mode is coded. It may be coded as autoconfigure or manual. It specifies if the LEC will autoconfigure (which means the LEC attaches to an LECS to discover the LES ATM address). For manual configuration, this parameter specifies the ATM address of the LES. This parameter is left blank if the Configure_mode is set to autoconfigure. The MAC address is optional.

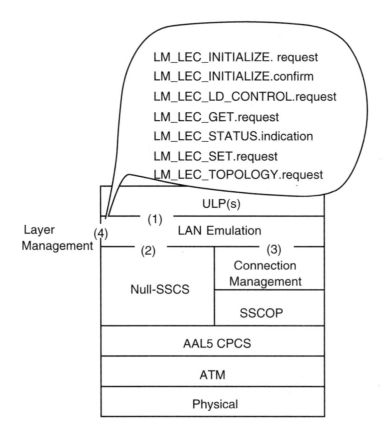

Figure 8–7   LE-layer management service specifications.

The LEC_proxy_class is coded as proxy or nonproxy. The Requested_LAN_type specifies the type of LAN that will be used for the operation. The Requested_max_frame_size can be set to 1516, 4544, 9234, or 18190 octets. The Request_ELAN_name parameter may be unspecified or contain the name of the emulated LAN the client wishes to join. Finally, the Join_time-out parameter contains a minimum time that the client should wait for a response to its join request or its configuration request.

The LM_LEC_INITIALIZE.confirm primitive confirms the request primitive and also indicates if the LECs interface is functional. It contains only one parameter, the Join_status. This parameter indicates if the initialization was a success or failure. If the Join_status indicates success, the LEC service user can begin sending and receiving traffic.

The LE client maintains a database of MAC addresses and route designators. The route designators contain the addresses that the LEC represents and, therefore, identifies the addresses for which it should receive frames. The LM_LEC_LD_CONTROL.request primitive is used to maintain this database. It allows entries to be added, deleted, or updated to the database. This primitive is coded as follows: LM_LEC_LD_CONTROL.request (LD_action, LD_type, LD_proxy_class, LAN_destination_address).

The LD_action parameter indicates if the address is to be deleted or added or if all entries are to be cleared. This later operation will clear all entries that match the specified LD_type and LD_proxy_class.

The LD_type parameter specifies multicast, unicast, or route designator.

The LD_proxy_class parameter specifies either proxy or local.

The LAN_destination_address parameter for a unicast or multicast LD_type is the conventional 48–bit MAC address. If the LD_type is a route designator, then the LAN_destination_address is a conventional 16-bit route designator that consists of the 12-bit segment ID and 4-bit bridge number.

The LE client contains a Management Information Base (MIB). The LM_LEC_GET.request is invoked by layer management to obtain information from the MIB. This primitive contains only one parameter, which is called the Attribute_id. This parameter can identify object identifiers in the MIB. The actual contents of this parameter are implementation specific.

In response to the previous primitive, the LE client sends the LM_LEC_STATUS.indication primitive with the status_report parameter. This parameter contains the information requested in the request primitive. Additionally, this primitive can be used by the LE client to provide layer management with alarms, statistics, error reports, and other functions.

The LM_LEC_SET.request primitive is used by layer management to control the behavior of the LE client. It actually operates on the LE client's MIB, which in turn will affect the operations of the LE client. The primitive contains the Attribute_id parameter discussed earlier and the Attribute_value parameter, which specifies the new value that is to be written into the MIB.

Finally, the LM_LEC_TOPOLOGY.request primitive is used to inform other LE clients about the change of a LAN topology. Its actual implementation varies but is used for example in transfer and bridge operations when a bridge sends out a configuration bridge protocol data unit (PDU). The primitive contains one parameter, the Topology_change_status, which is coded to indicate topology change or no topology change.

The receipt of this primitive from layer management requires the LE client to send a topology request frame to the LES.

DATA FRAMES

The two data frames used in LAN emulation are shown in Figure 8–8. The top frame shows the IEEE 802.3/Ethernet frame and the lower frame shows the IEEE 802.5 frame.[2]

For the top frame, the minimum AAL5 SDU length is 62 octets. The LAN emulation header (LE header) is 2 octets in length and contains either the LEC id of the sending LEC or is set to all 0s. The next fields con-

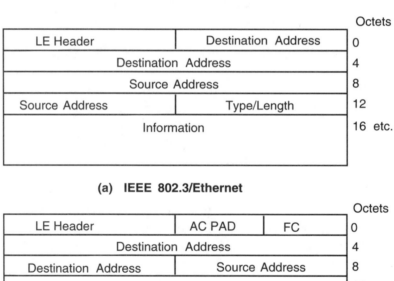

(a) IEEE 802.3/Ethernet

(b) IEEE 802.5

Figure 8–8   Data frame format.

[2]Part of the LANE specification uses the notations X"——" or X—— to depict hex values.

tain the destination and source MAC addresses followed by the type/length fields.

LAN emulation must support both LLC frames and Ethernet frames.

The second format in the lower frame of Figure 8–8 is intended for token ring LANs. For this frame, the minimum AAL5 SDU length is 16 octets. The AC pad octet is not used in this specification. Furthermore, with 802.5 networks, only LLC frames are supported. Consequently, the FC octet must adhere to the IEEE 802.5 1992 specification.

Figure 8–9 and Table 8–5 show the syntax and format for LAN emulation control frames. All frames use the structure shown in this figure, with the exception of the READY_IND and READY_QUERY frames, which use a format described later.

Type/Length (TL) Operations[3]

Since LAN emulation supports IEEE 802.2 (LLC) and Ethertype encapsulations, a convention is established on how the TL information is used. The rules can be summarized as follows:[4]

				Octets
Marker = X"FF00"		Protocol =X"01"	Version = "01"	0
Op-Code		Status		4
Transaction-ID				8
Requester-LECID		Flags		12
Source LAN Destination				16
Target LAN Destination (see Table 8–6)				24
Source ATM Address				32
LAN-Type	Maximum-Frame-Size	Number-TLVS	ELAN-Name-Size	52
Target-ATM-Address				56
ELAN-Name				76
TLVs Begin				108

Figure 8–9   Control frame format.

---

[3]Some of the specifications in this book use the term type, length, value (TLV) in place of type, length.

[4]These rules also apply to MPOA; see Chapter 11.

Table 8–5   Table for Figure 8-9

Marker	Control frame = X"FF00"	2
Protocol	ATM LAN Emulation protocol = X"01"	1
Version	ATM LAN Emulation protocol version = X"01"	1
OP-Code	Control frame type	2
Status	Always X"0000" in requests	2
Transaction ID	Arbitrary value supplied by the requester and returned by the responder to allow the receiver to discriminate between different responses.	4
Requester-LECID	LECID of LE Client sending the request (X"0000" if unknown).	2
Flags	Bit flags:	2
	X"0001" = Remote Address (LE_ARP_RESPONSE) X"0080" = Proxy Flag (LE_JOIN_REQUEST) X"0100" = Topology Change (LE_TOPOLOGY_REQUEST)	
	Meaning of remainder of fields depends on OP-Code.	92

- For Ethernet traffic, the Ethertype field is placed in the TL field
- For LLC traffic:
  - Frames less than 1536 octets (including the LLC field and data but not including padding and FCS) must have this length placed in the TL field, followed by the LLC data.
  - Longer frames must have a 0 in the TL field, followed by the LLC data.

Table 8–7 shows the coding rules for the status field that resides in the header shown earlier. This field is not used in a request frame, it is used in a response frame to provide the status of an ongoing operation. As Table 8–7 shows, most of the status information deals with identify-

Table 8–6   Rules for Coding the LAN Destination Fields

Name	Function	Octets
TAG	X"0000" = not present X"0001" = MAC address X"0002" = Route Descriptor	2
MAC address	6-octet MAC address if MAC address specified	6
RESERVED	0, if Route Descriptor specified	4
Route Descriptor	If Route Descriptor specified	2

Table 8–7 Control Frame Status Field

(dec)	Name	Meaning	Responses
0	Success	Successful response.	All responses
1	Version not supported	VERSION field of request contains a value higher than that supported by the responder.	All responses
2	Invalid request parameters	The parameters given are incompatible with the ELAN.	All responses
4	Duplicate LAN Destination registration	SOURCE-LAN-DESTINATION duplicates a previously registered LAN address.	Join or Register
5	Duplicate ATM address	SOURCE-ATM-ADDRESS duplicates a previously registered ATM address.	Join or Register
6	Insufficient resources to grant request	Responder is unable to grant request for reasons such as insufficient table space or ability to establish VCCs.	Configure, Join or Register
7	Access denied	Request denied for security reasons.	Configure or Join
8	Invalid REQUESTOR-ID	LECID field is not zero (Configure or Join) or is not LE Client's LECID (others).	Configure, Join, Register, Unregister, ARP
9	Invalid LAN destination	LAN destination is a multicast address or on an Ethernet/802.3 ELAN, a Route Descriptor.	Configure, Join, Register, ARP, Flush
10	Invalid ATM address	Source or target ATM address not in a recognizable format.	Configure, Join, Register, ARP, Flush
20	No configuration	LE client is not recognized.	Configure
21	LE_CONFIGURE Error	Parameters supplied give conflicting answers. May also be used to refuse service without giving a specific reason.	Configure
22	Insufficient information	LE client has not provided sufficient information to allow the LECS to assign it to a specific ELAN.	Configure

**Table 8–8   Rules for Coding
the OP-CODE Field**

Value	Function
X"0001"	LE_CONFIGURE_REQUEST
X"0101"	LE_CONFIGURE_RESPONSE
X"0002"	LE_JOIN_REQUEST
X"0102"	LE_JOIN_RESPONSE
X"0003"	READY_QUERY
X"0103"	READY_IND
X"0004"	LE_REGISTER_REQUEST
X"0104"	LE_REGISTER_RESPONSE
X"0005"	LE_UNREGISTER_REQUEST
X"0105"	LE_UNREGISTER_RESPONSE
X"0006"	LE_ARP_REQUEST
X"0106"	LE_ARP_RESPONSE
X"0007"	LE_FLUSH_REQUEST
X"0107"	LE_FLUSH_RESPONSE
X"0008"	LE_NARP_REQUEST
X"0108"	Undefined
X"0009"	LE_TOPOLOGY_REQUEST
X"0109"	Undefined

ing problems that occurred during the exchange of control frames. Table 8–7 shows the name of each status value, a brief description of its meaning, and which response frames carries this field.

The OP-CODE field in the control frame header is coded to identify the type frame. The field is coded in accordance with the convention shown in Table 8–8.

SUMMARY

The LAN emulation service specifications define operations between the layers in a node while OSI-based SAPs and primitives are used.

LANE defines four sets of primitives: (1) LAN emulation—ULP service specifications, (2) LAN emulation—AAL service specifications, (3) LAN emulation—AAL service specifications, and (4) LAN emulation—layer management service specifications. In addition, LANE specifies the formats, syntaxes and contents of the PDUs.

9

Configuration, Registration, and ARP Procedures and LNNI

T his chapter discusses the major housekeeping operations employed in a LANE. The focus is on (1) how the LANE is initially configured, (2) how the clients and servers register themselves and their respective addresses, and (3) how the LANE ARP is employed for address resolution.

This chapter delves into these three operations with several examples that are amplified with an analysis of the various PDU formats (LANE uses the term frame to describe basic MAC frames as well as LANE PDUs).

The concluding part of the chapter introduces the LAN Emulation Network-Network Interface (LNNI). The explanation of LNNI is brief because it uses many of the LNNI concepts.

THE CONFIGURE OPERATION

The configure operation was introduced in Chapter 7. Recall that it is used for the LE client to discover the LE service. Upon completion of the configuration phase, the LE client will be identified with a unique LE client identifier (LECID) and a ELAN name. In addition, the LE client now knows the emulated LAN's type (i.e., Ethernet), and the emulated LAN's maximum frame size.

Figure 9–1 shows some of the key information in the configure request and response messages that are exchanged by the LEC and LES. It will be helpful to consult Table 9–1 during this discussion. The MAC ad-

Table 9–1   A Configuration Frame Format

Name	Function	Size
Marker	Control Frame = X"FF00"	2
Protocol	ATM LAN Emulation protocol = X"01"	1
Version	ATM LAN Emulation protocol version = X"01"	1
OP-Code	Type of request: X"0001" LE_CONFIGURE_REQUEST X"0101" LE_CONFIGURE_RESPONSE	2
Status	Always X"0000" in requests. See Status field for a list of values.	2
Transaction ID	Arbitrary value supplied by the requester and returned by the responder.	4
Requester-LECID	Always X"0000" in requests, ignored on response.	2
Flags	Always X"0000" when sent, ignored on receipt	2
Source-LAN-Destination	MAC address or Route Descriptor of prospective LE Client. May be encoded as "not present."	8
Target-LAN-Destination	Always X"0000" when sent, ignored on receipt.	8
Source-ATM-Address	Primary ATM address of prospective LE Client for which information is requested	20
LAN-Type	X"00" unspecified, X"01" Ethernet/IEEE 802.3, X"02" IEEE 802.5	1
Maximum-Frame-Size	X"00" unspecified, X"01" 1516, X"02" 4544, X"03" 9234, X"04" 18190	1
Number-TLVS	Number of Type/Length/Value elements encoded in Request/Response.	1
ELAN-Name-Size	Number of octets in ELAN-Name (may be 0).	1
Target-ATM-Address	ATM Address of the LE Server to be used for the LE Client described in the request if Configure Response and Status = "Success," else X'00'	20
ELAN-Name	Name of emulated LAN.	32
ITEM_1-Type	Three octets of OUI, one octet identifier	4
ITEM_1-Length	Length in octets of Value field. Minimum = 0.	1
ITEM_-Value	See Table 9–2	Var.
Etc.		

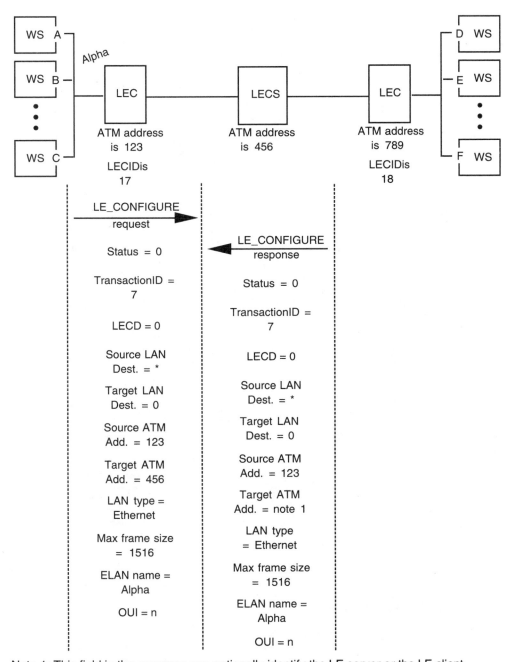

Note 1: This field in the response can optionally identify the LE server or the LE client

Figure 9–1   A configure operation.

dresses are not pertinent for this operation, since it entails only the registration of ATM addresses. The * notation in the Source-LAN-Destination field means this field can be coded as "not present." Also, the LANE specification uses a prefix X to connote hex values; other systems described in this book use 0x.

The LEC wishes to register its ATM address (123) with the LECS. It also registers the name of an ELAN (alpha) and the characteristics of the LAN itself (LAN type = Ethernet; maximum frame size = 1516 octets). The target ATM address (456) identifies the LECS through which this configuration is to occur.

The status field is always x0000 in the request message. Its contents in the response depend upon the outcome of the configuration operations (see Table 8–7 of Chapter 8). The transaction ID (7) is selected by the requestor and used again in the response to correlate the request and response messages.

After this exchange, the LECS knows about the ELAN alpha and its associated ATM addresses at the LEC. As noted in note 1 of Figure 9–1, the LECS also informs the LEC of its LES.

Table 9–1 shows the content and syntax for the configuration frame format. As the OP code indicates, it can carry a request or response frame. Other fields in the frame are used to identify the type of LAN, the maximum frame sized to be used, and the ATM address of the LE server that the LE client considers appropriate. This address (if appropriate) is acknowledged by the LE server in its response to the LE client. Notice also that the name of the emulated LAN is included as well as the organization unique ID (OUI, explained in Chapter 2).

Table 9–2 provides more information of the contents of the configuration response frame. It deals with numerous operations that will go into effect on this connection. The description of each of these fields are summarized in the left column. The type/length/value fields are coded to convey this information to the LE client.

THE JOIN OPERATION

Figure 9–2 provides an example of the join operations, which is used by the LE client to establish a connection with the LE server to store the operating parameters of the emulated LAN. The join operation also permits the LE client to register one MAC address with the LE server. In this example, the source LAN destination address A is being registered and bound to the source ATM address of 123.

Table 9–2   Configuration Response Frame (see Appendix C for the Cn parameters)

Item	Type	Length	Reference/Value/Units
Control Time-out	00-A0-3E-01	2	C7/in seconds
Maximum Unknown Frame Count	00-A0-3E-02	2	C10
Maximum Unknown Frame Time	00-A0-3E-03	2	C11/in seconds
VCC Time-out Period	00-A0-3E-04	4	C12/in seconds
Maximum Retry Count	00-A0-3E-05	2	C13
Aging Time	00-A0-3E-06	4	C17/in seconds
Forward Delay Time	00-A0-3E-07	2	C18/in seconds
Expected LE_ARP Response Time	00-A0-3E-08	2	C20/in seconds
Flush Time-out	00-A0-3E-09	2	C21/in seconds
Path Switching Delay	00-A0-3E-0A	2	C22/in seconds
Local Segment ID	00-A0-3E-0B	2	C23
Mcast Send VCC Type	00-A0-3E-0C	2	C24:
			X0000 Best Effort: LE Client should set the BE flag. Peak Cell Rates should be line rate.
			X0001 Variable: LE Client should provide a Sustained Cell Rate.[1]
			X0002 Constant: LE Client should provide a Peak and a Sustained Cell Rate.[1]
Mcast Send VCC AvgRate	00-A0-3E-0D	4	C25/in cells per second
Mcast Send VCC PeakRate	00-A0-3E-0E	4	C26/in cells per second
Connection Completion Timer	00-A0-3E-0F	2	C28/in seconds

[1]Where: 00-A0-3E is the ATM forum OUI.

The LE server returns the response to the LE client, which is coded in the status field to acknowledge or deny the join request.

It is evident that the LANE messages are similar for configurations, joins (and others). Therefore and hereafter, I will not describe each field in these messages, but refer you to a table that describes the fields.

Figure 9–2 shows the principal fields that are coded in the messages. Other fields reside in this messages and are explained in Table 9–3.

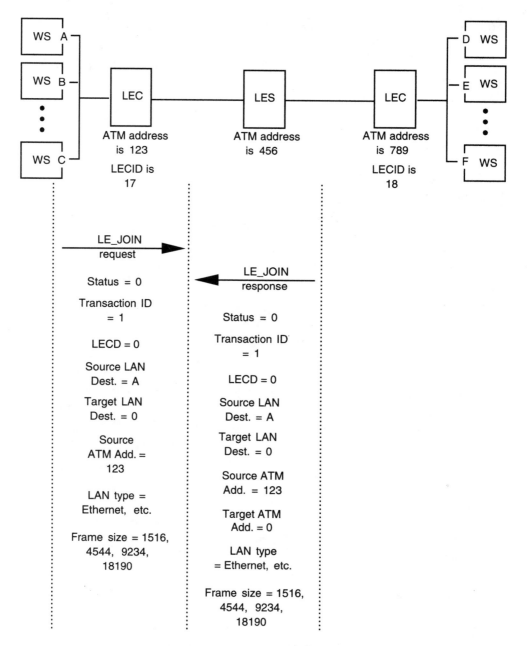

Figure 9–2 The join operation.

Table 9–3   Join Frame Format

Name	Function	Size
Marker	Control Frame = X"FF00"	2
Protocol	ATM LAN Emulation protocol = X"01"	1
Version	ATM LAN Emulation protocol version = X"01"	1
OP-Code	Type of request: X"0002" LE_JOIN_REQUEST X"0102" LE_JOIN_RESPONSE	2
Status	Always X"0000" in requests. See Status table for a list of values.	2
Transaction ID	Arbitrary value supplied by the requester and returned by the responder.	4
Requester-LECID	Assigned LECID of joining client if join response and STATUS = "Success", else X"0000".	2
Flags	Each bit of the FLAGS field has a separate meaning if set.	2
	X"0080" is the Proxy Flag: LE Client serves non-registered MAC addresses and therefore wishes to receive LE_ARP requests for non-registered LAN destinations.	
Source-LAN-Destination	Optional MAC address to register as a pair with the SOURCE_ATM_ADDRESS.	8
Target-LAN-Destination	Always X"00" when sent, ignored on receipt.	8
Source-ATM-Address	Primary ATM address of LE Client issuing join request.	20
LAN-Type	X"00" unspecified, X"01" Ethernet/IEEE 802.3, X"02" IEEE 802.5	1
Maximum-Frame-Size	X"00" unspecified, X"01" 1516, X"02" 4544, X"03" 9234, X"04" 18190	1
Number-TLVS	Always X"00" when sent, ignored on receipt.	1
ELAN-Name-Size	Number of octets in ELAN-Name. X"00" indicates empty ELAN-Name.	1
Target-ATM-Address	Always X"00" when sent, ignored on receipt.	20
ELAN-Name	Name of emulated LAN.	32
	Expresses LE Client's preference in LE_JOIN_REQUEST, specifies name of LAN joined in successful LE_JOIN_RESPONSE, else not used. Format is SNMPv2 DisplayString.	

THE REGISTRATION OPERATION

Figure 9–3 provides an example of registration operation. This procedure is used by the LE client to provide the LE server with LAN destination/ATM address pairs that have not yet been registered. The join procedure may have these addresses established. However, as new workstations are added to a LAN, the registration procedure becomes a useful tool for bringing all entities up to date about the new workstations.

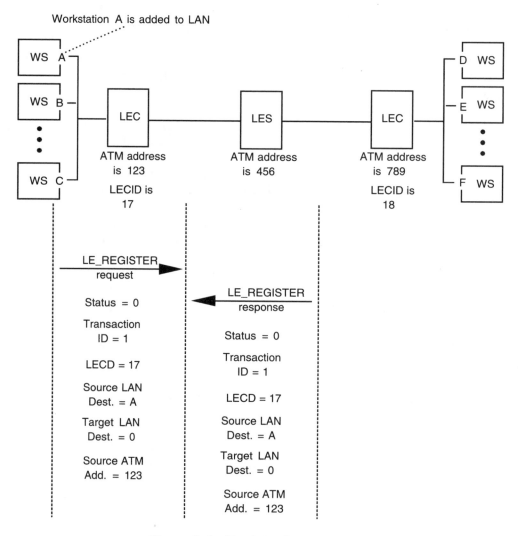

Figure 9–3   Registration example.

As with the join operation, this example shows that the registration is binding MAC address A to ATM address 123 and is confirmed by the LES returning a register response frame to the LEC.

An LE client may also request the LE server remove an address pair with an unregister request frame (which is not shown in Figure 9–3). In turn, the LE server will respond with an unregister response that will confirm or deny the unregistration request.

Registration Frame Format

Table 9–4 shows the content and syntax of the registration and unregistration frames. As the OP code indicates, this frame can be coded as a request or a response. The Source-LAN-Destination and Source-ATM-Address fields provide the values for the address pairs.

Table 9–4   Registration Frame Format

Name	Function	Size
Marker	Control Frame = X"FF00"	2
Protocol	ATM LAN Emulation protocol = X"01"	1
Version	ATM LAN Emulation protocol version = X"01"	1
OP-Code	Type of request: X"0004" LE_REGISTER_REQUEST X"0104" LE_REGISTER_RESPONSE X"0005" LE_UNREGISTER_REQUEST X"0105" LE_UNREGISTER_RESPONSE	2
Status	Always X"0000" in requests. In Responses: See Table 8–7 in Chapter 8 for a list of values.	2
Transaction ID	Arbitrary value supplied by the requester and returned by the responder.	4
Requester-LECID	LECID of LE client issuing the register or unregister request and returned by the responder.	2
Flags	Always X"00" when sent, ignored on receipt.	2
Source-LAN-Destination	Unicast MAC address or Route Descriptor LE client is attempting to register.	8
Target-LAN-Destination	Always X"00" when sent, ignored on receipt.	8
Source-ATM-Address	An ATM address of LE Client issuing the register or unregister request.	20
Reserved	Always X"00" when sent, ignored on receipt.	56

THE LANE ADDRESS RESOLUTION PROTOCOL

Previous chapters in this book have described the operations of ARP. In Chapter 2, we introduced the use of ARP in ATM and Frame Relay operations. This chapter picks up on earlier discussions and focuses in more detail on the LAN emulation ARP.

THE ARP FRAMES

Four frames are employed for address resolution. The LE_ARP_REQUEST frame is used to associate the ATM address with a MAC address or a route descriptor. This frame is sent by an LE client.

In turn, the LE_ARP_RESPONSE frame is sent by either an LE client or an LE server in response the to LE_ARP_REQUEST frame.

The LE_NARP_REQUEST frame is sent by an LE client when changes occur in the addresses associated with the LE client.

The LE_TOPOLOGY_REQUEST frame is sent by either an LE server or an LE client whenever changes to network topologies occur.

LE CLIENT USE OF ARP

All ARP requests and responses emanating from the LE client must be sent over the control direct VCC (see Figure 9–4). In turn, receiving requests or responses may arrive either on the control direct VCC or the control distribute VCC.

To prevent uncontrolled operations in the emulated LAN, an LE client may not participate in ARP operations until it has joined the emulated LAN.

Upon receiving an LE_ARP_REQUEST frame, the LE client examines the requested addresses in the frame and checks these addresses against its local addressees. If it finds a match in (a) local unicast MAC address, (b) route descriptors, or (c) remote unicast MAC addresses, it must respond with an LE_ARP_RESPONSE frame. It is not allowed to respond to any other addresses.

The LE client can obtain the address of the broadcast and unknown server by sending an LE_ARP_REQUEST for the broadcast group address.

In an SVC environment, when the LE client receives a response that resolves an unresolved cache entry and there is no existing data direct VCC, a setup operation must be initiated by this client.

Another rule is important regarding the frequency that the LE client can transmit ARP requests, The rule is that these requests cannot be sent to the same destination more than once every second.

Many ARP implementations allow a node to listen passively to the ARP responses going across a communications channel. Thereby, learning about address mappings. Some systems call this system gleaning. This specification calls it eavesdropping and the LE client is permitted to update its cache by eavesdropping the responses.

LE SERVER USE OF ARP

The LE server must adhere to a set of rules also. First, it can only process request and response frames that are received on a control direct VCC. It is not permitted to process these frames if they are received on any other VCC. In turn, it sends requests and responses to an LE client on a control direct VCC or on a control distribute VCC.

The LE server is not allowed to service requests for an unregistered LAN destination—only registered MAC addresses are supported. Furthermore, the LE server is not allowed to flood requests further to LE clients if it responds to the request. In contrast, if it does not respond to the request, it must forward that request to LE clients.

As I just mentioned, an unfulfilled request can be sent to other clients and is also forwarded back to the requesting LE client.

The LE server also processes topology request frames. Upon receiving a topology request frame from any client, it must forward this frame to all LE clients. This operation supports the concept of flooding topology information throughout the emulated LAN. The LE server also issues topology requests and need not rely on the LE client to initiate this action.

EXAMPLE OF ARP OPERATIONS

Figure 9–4 shows how the ARP operation is invoked to obtain an ATM address pertaining to a destination MAC address. Workstation A transmits a frame with destination address D. Upon arriving at the LEC, it is discovered that address D and its associated ATM address is not known. Therefore, this LEC forms an ARP request message and transmits this message to its LES. Since a previous join or registration operation had resulted in MAC address D and its associated registration address of 789 being registered with the LES, this LES can satisfy the ARP

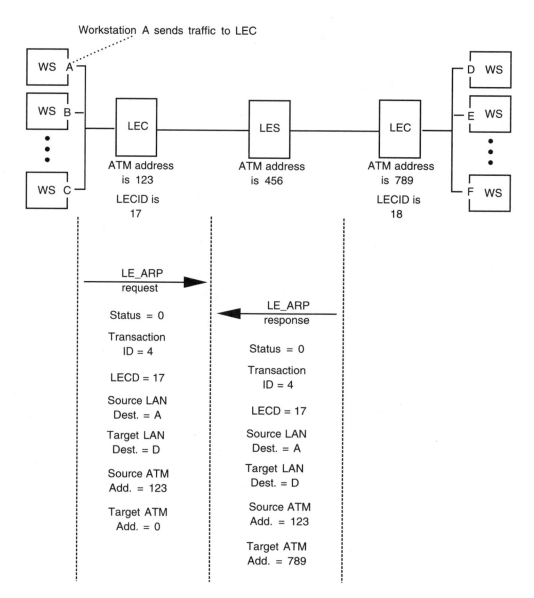

Figure 9–4　Example of the ARP operations.

request with the ARP response, which informs the requesting LEC that ATM address 789 is associated with the destination MAC address.

ARP Frame Format

Table 9–5 describes the format and contents of the LE_ARP frame. As a reminder from previous discussions, these frames are coded in one of two formats.

The first format is coded as the LE_ARP_REQUEST frame, which is sent by the LE client and is used to determine the ATM address associated with a MAC address or a route descriptor.

Table 9–5   The LE_ARP Frame Format

Name	Function	Size
Marker	Control Frame = X"FF00"	2
Protocol	ATM LAN Emulation protocol = X"01"	1
Version	ATM LAN Emulation protocol version = X"01"	1
OP-Code	Type of request: X"0006" LE_ARP_REQUEST X"0106" LE_ARP_RESPONSE	2
Status	Always X"0000" in requests. See STATUS values in the control frame for a list of values.	2
Transaction ID	Arbitrary value supplied by the requester.	4
Requester-LECID	LECID of LE client issuing the LE_ARP request	2
Flags	Each bit of the FLAGS field has a separate meaning if set: X"0001" Remote address. The TARGET-LAN-DESTINATION is not registered with the LE server.	2
Source-LAN-Destination	Source MAC address from data frame that triggered this LE_ARP sequence. May be encoded with "not present" LAN destination tag.	8
Target-LAN-Destination	Destination unicast MAC address or next Route Descriptor for which an ATM address is being sought.	8
Source-ATM-Address	ATM address of originator of LE_ARP request.	20
Reserved	Always X"00" when sent, ignored on receipt.	4
Target-ATM-Address	X"00" in LE_ARP request. ATM address of LE client responsible for target LAN destination in LE_ARP response.	20
Reserved	Always X"00" when sent, ignored on receipt.	32

The second format is coded as the LE_ARP_RESPONSE frame, which is sent by the LE server or LE client to provide the information that was requested in the LE_ARP_REQUEST.

LE_NARP Frame Format

Table 9–6 shows the format for the LE_NARP frame. This frame is generated by an LE client to inform other clients that a remote LAN-ATM address binding has changed. The binding that is changed in coded in the Target-LAN-Destination field, and the Target-ATM-Address field. The address of the LE client that sends this frame is contained in the Source-ATM-Address field.

In addition to changing the binding, this frame also informs its recipients that the client at the Source-ATM-Address is now representing the LAN destination (that is, the address in the Target-LAN-Destination field).

Table 9–6   LE_NARP Frame Format

Name	Function	Size
Marker	Control Frame = X"FF00"	2
Protocol	ATM LAN Emulation protocol = X"01"	1
Version	ATM LAN Emulation protocol version = X"01"	1
OP-Code	Type of request: X"0008" LE_NARP_REQUEST	2
Status	Always X"0000".	2
Transaction ID	Arbitrary value supplied by the requester.	4
Requester-LECID	LECID of LE client issuing the LE_NARP request.	2
Flags	Always X"00".	2
Source-LAN-Destination	Not used. Encoded as X'00'.	8
Target-LAN-Destination	Destination unicast MAC address or next Route Descriptor for which the target ATM address no longer applies.	8
Source-ATM-Address	ATM address of originator of LE_NARP request.	20
Reserved	Always X"00" when sent, ignored on receipt.	4
Target-ATM-Address	ATM address of LE client which was previously representing the target LAN destination.	20
Reserved	Always X"00" when sent, ignored on receipt.	32

LE_Topology_Request Frame Format

The format for the LE_Topology_Request frame is shown in Table 9–7. This frame is sent only on a network that is using the IEEE 802.1D transparent bridge operations. The LE_client that is acting as the transparent bridge must sent one LE_Topology_Request frame to its LE server for every configuration BPDU it sends to the BUS.

LAN EMULATION NETWORK-NETWORK INTERFACE (LNNI)

The ELAN defines a single point of service for the LEC and LECS, which can result in bottlenecks and outage (from a single point of failure).

To address these problems, the ATM Forum has published the LAN Emulation Network-Network Interface (LNNI). It is quite similar to LANE and LUNI, but has the following additional capabilities:

- Multiple LECs are permitted and can be located in geographically dispersed locations. These LECs appear as one service (a virtual ELAN)
- Thus, LNNI is scaleable, and permits many MAC nodes, LANS, and ELAN servers to interact
- The server cache synchronization protocol (SCSP) is used to keep all LNNI servers and clients updated with consistent and correct information.

Table 9–7 The Topology Request Frame Format

Name	Function	Size
Marker	Control Frame = X"FF00"	2
Protocol	ATM LAN Emulation protocol = X"01"	1
Version	ATM LAN Emulation protocol version = X"01"	1
OP-Code	Type of request: X"0009" LE_TOPOLOGY_REQUEST	2
Status	Always X"0000".	2
Transaction ID	Arbitrary value supplied by the requester.	4
Requester-LECID	LECID of LE client issuing the Topology Change request	2
Flags	Each bit of the FLAGS field has a separate meaning if set: X"0100" Topology Change Flag. A network topology change is in progress.	2
Reserved	Always X"00" when sent, ignored on receipt.	92

LNNI uses the VCCs and 802.1 spanning tree operations that are used in LUNI. Most of the LUNI messages (registration, etc.) are also used

Some of the deficiencies of LNNI are:

- Unknown unicast traffic is broadcasted throughout the LNNI spanning tree, which may create excessive traffic (broadcast storms) and overload servers
- LNNI is still an overlay network, treating ATM as a simple layer 2 service, and thus does not avail itself of the full features of ATM

Nonetheless, LNNI is a positive and welcome addition to the ATM internetworking family and a substantial enhancement to LUNI.

SUMMARY

In Chapter 9, three operations have been addressed: the configuration operation, the join operation, and the registration operation.

We learned that the configuration operation allows the LE client to obtain an ATM address of the LE server. The join operation supports the connection to the LE server, the exchange of operating parameters, and the registration of MAC addresses; and the registration operation allows for additional MAC addresses to be registered.

We have also covered three major facets of ARP. First, the ARP messages are used to bind a MAC address to an ATM address. Second, prior registration procedures may reduce the amount of ARP traffic that must be exchanged; and third, ARP messages are also used to update MAC address/ATM address bindings.

10

Next Hop Resolution
Protocol (NHRP)

This chapter discusses the Non-Broadcast Multi-Access (NBMA) Next Hop Resolution Protocol (NHRP). The term NBMA refers to a nonbroadcast subnetwork. This type of network does not operate with broadcasting operations because it is inherently non-broadcast (i.e., an X.25 network) or because it is a broadcast network but broadcasting is not feasible because of the size of the network. Hereafter, I refer to the term NRHP without the term NBMA in front of it.

The information contained in this chapter provides a summary of the NHRP specification (NHRPv8). This specification is still a draft but is probably the last one before going to RFC status. Be aware that the final RFC will likely have changes, but the summary of NHRP in this chapter should closely resemble the final specification.

PURPOSE OF NHRP

The purpose of NHRP is to discover and correlate a layer 3 (the internetwork layer address) and the NBMA subnetwork address of the NBMA *next hop* to a destination station. The term NBMA subnetwork address refers to the underlying layer beneath the internetworking layer. Examples of NBMA subnetwork addresses are X.25 addresses, ATM addresses, and SMDS addresses.[1] Examples of internetwork layer addresses are the IP address, the Connectionless Network Layer Protocol (CLNP) address, and the IPX address.

If the L_3 destination address is connected to the NBMA subnetwork, then the next hop is directly to the destination station. If the destination is not connected to the NBMA subnetwork, then the next hop must be to an egress router that can reach the destination station. Ideally, this router is the best path to the destination, but NHRP is not designed to resolve address mappings or path analysis beyond the NBMA subnetwork. Of course, for a system to function properly, conventional route discovery protocols should be employed between NBMA subnetworks to find these paths. Notwithstanding, NHRP can find an egress router by its own operations and does not have to rely on other discovery protocols, even though ARP can co-exist with NHRP.

NHRP is also designed to reduce or eliminate extra router hops that are part of the conventional LIS model. Recall that classical IP over ATM does not permit bypassing intermediate routers on different logical IP subnetworks (LISs) (that are connected even to the same ATM network). NHRP eliminates this restriction.

In effect, NHRP is based on the classical IP model but:

- uses the concept of a NBMA in place of the LIS
- uses the concept of an NHRP server (NHS) in place of a conventional ARP server

MODELING THE NBMA NETWORK

NBMA establishes two methods to model the NBMA network. The first method is quite similar to the model in RFC 1577, Classical IP and ARP over ATM, which is described in Chapter 2. This method uses logically independent IP subnets (LISs) with the following attributes:

---

[1]Strictly speaking, this definition of an NBMA subnetwork addresses is not correct, although it is used throughout the NHRP specifications. X.25 is a internetwork layer operation but the idea behind the NHRP is to define the conventional internetworking layer (layer 3) to operate over the NBMA subnetwork. So, for X.25 we could have two layer 3 protocols involved in the process with, say, IP running on top of X.25.

- LIS members have the same IP address and address mask.
- LIS members are all connected to the same NBMA subnetwork.
- All stations outside the LIS must be accessed through a router.

With RFC 1577, address resolution is resolved only when the next hop address of the destination station is a member of the same LIS as the source station. If this situation does not exist, the source station forwards traffic to a router that may belong to multiple LISs. In such a case, the hop-by-hop address resolution may result in multiple hops through the NBMA subnetwork.

The second method to model the NBMA is to use the concept of local address groups (LAGs).[2] The LAG concept moves away from routing based on addressing toward routing based on quality of service features (such as delay, throughput, etc.). This concept represents the overall thrust of advanced networks: implementing sophisticated routing and route discovery mechanisms that are responsive to end user applications' requirements.

NHRP Operations

Some of the concepts of NHRP are closely related to LANE (discussed earlier in this book in regards to the use of clients and servers) (see Figure 10–1). In this technology, the server is called the next hop server (NHS). Its responsibility is to perform the next hop resolution protocol within the NBMA subnetwork. The term client refers to the next hop client (NHC). The client initiates NHRP requests to the next hop server in order to obtain correlations between layer 3 addresses and NBMA subnetwork addresses.

In Figure 10–1, three NBMA networks are connected through an ATM backbone. The routers supporting these networks are configured with next hop client (NHC) capabilities. The next hop server (NHS) is also connected to the ATM backbone.

In general, NHRP operates as follows:

- The NHC sends a request to its NHS to resolve an IP address to an ATM address in order to setup an ATM connection
- The NHS responds with the mapping information. If it does not know the IP/ATM address relationship, it sends the query toward

---

[2]Further information on the concept of local address groups can be found in a Pending RFCxxxx, titled: "Local/Remote Forwarding Decision and Switched Data Link Subnetworks," authored by Yakov Rekhter and Dilip Kandlur.

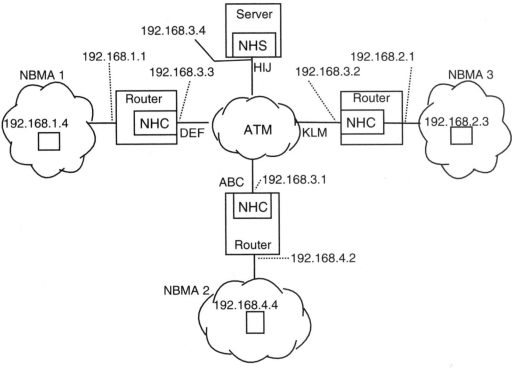

Figure 10–1   The NBMA configuration.

the destination address based on routes discovered by conventional route discovery mechanisms (for example, OSPF).

- As the query proceeds along its way, any intermediate (transit) NHS may service the query if the NHS has the information in its cache (from previous NHRP messages).

- Otherwise, the query will arrive at the NHS just before the destination NHC and this NHS responds to the query (this NHS is called the serving NHS).

- The response is sent back on the same path as the query, which allows the transit NHSs to update their cache.

- Upon receiving the response the NHC has enough information to send an ATM Q.2931 setup message to the ATM network to setup an SVC.

The NHSs must be capable of answering next hop resolution requests that find the ATM node that services a L_3 address. These NHSs are configured to serve a set of destination hosts, which may be connected directly to the NBMA subnetwork (but need not be). In addition to running NHRP within their respective subnetworks, the NHSs may also participate beyond their subnetworks to disseminate routing information beyond the NBMA boundaries through conventional route discovery protocols. The NHS can also support conventional ARP services.

In order to resolve address mapping requests, the NHS maintains a cache known as next hop resolution cache. The cache is a table of address mappings that correlate internetwork layer addresses to NBMA subnetwork layer addresses. Like most ARP-type operations, the table is built from the replies to next hop resolution requests or from eavesdropping registration packets that establish these correlations.

Like LANE, registration operations are evoked when a node decides to be part of NHRP. The registering station sends an NHRP registration message to an NHS, which contains the NBMA information about that station. Thereafter, the NHS is responsible for making this information known to other NHSs or NHCs.

One more point: A host or router can be configured as an NHS. If it is not so configured, it must be able to identify the NHS that is configured to serve it.

EXAMPLES OF NBMA OPERATIONS

For this example (using Figure 10–1), let us assume that a station residing in NBMA 1 receives traffic that requires the resolution of an NBMA address to get the traffic to its destination (192.168.4.4) in NBMA 2. In this context, a station can be a router or a host computer that has an NHRP capability. Upon receiving a datagram from host 192.168.1.4, a next hop client (NHC, which is typically a router with HNC capabilities) determines the next hop to the final destination station through normal routing operations. If the next hop is reachable through the NHC's NBMA interface, the NHC constructs a Next Hop Resolution Request packet that contains (1) the internetwork layer target address (192.168.4.4), (2) the internetwork layer source address (192.168.3.3, which is called the next hop resolution request initiator), and (3) the NHC's ATM address (DEF in this example).

The NHC in NBMA 1 sends a Next Hop Resolution Request message to its NHS, using the source NBMA address of DEF. This message arrives at the NHS, which is identified with an ATM address of HIJ.

The NHS with address HIJ checks to determine if it serves station 192.168.4.4 (the subnet 192.168.4). By "serve," it is meant that station HIJ has a next hop entry in its next hop resolution table for subnet 192.168.4. If HIJ does not serve the destination subnet, it forwards the next hop resolution request message to another NHS.

Since NHS HIJ serves subnet 192.168.4, it constructs a positive next hop resolution reply message that contains either the next hop internetwork layer address of a directly attached station, or the internetwork layer address of the egress router through which traffic can be forwarded. For this example, the second option is executed, since the destination address in on another NBMA network. Therefore, the NHRP reply informs NHC 192.168.3.3/DEF that the next hop is node 192.168.3.1/ABC.

In summary, the request message contains:

1. Source NBMA address   = DEF
2. Source protocol address   = 192.168.3.3
3. Destination protocol address = 192.168.4.4

The reply message contains:

1. Source NBMA address   = DEF
2. Source protocol address   = 192.168.3.3
3. Destination protocol address = 192.168.4.4
4. Next hop NBMA address   = ABC
5. Next hop protocol address   = 192.168.3.1

Authoritative and Nonauthoritative Replies

NHRP replies are either authoritative or nonauthoritative. If an NHS serves the node associated with the destination address, its reply is authoritative. Otherwise, the reply is nonauthoritative in this regard: An intermediate NHS that receives a next hop resolution reply may cache this information. Upon receiving a subsequent next hop resolution request, it may respond with the cached reply, but it must be identified as nonauthoritative.

Restrictions on the Messages

NHRP request and replies are not allowed to cross the borders of a logical NBMA subnetwork. All L_3 traffic into and out of the NBMA subnetwork must pass through a L_3 router at the NBMA border.

Station Configurations

An NHRP station must be configured with the NBMA address of its NHS. The NHS(s) may also be the station's default router. It is possible for a station to be attached to more than one subnetwork; if so, the station must be configured to receive routing information from all NHSs in order to determine which L_3 addresses are reachable through which subnetworks.

A MORE DETAILED EXAMPLE

The next example, in Figure 10–2, provides more detailed information on the contents of the NHRP Next Hop Resolution Request and Reply messages. We assume the NHC with addresses DEF/192.168.3.3 receives a datagram destined for station 192.168.2.3 that is located in NBMA 2. NHC DEF sends an NHRP request message to the NHS whose address is HIJ/192.168.3.4. Notice that the request message has the destination protocol address coded as the target protocol address of 192.168.2.3.

The NHS NHRP tables reveal that subnet 192.168.2 is reachable through NHC KLM/192.168.3.2. Therefore, the NHS sends back the NHRP response message with the next hop fields coded to identify the egress router to NBMA 2. This router is identified with addresses KLM/192.168.3.2. This NHRP response provides sufficient information for NHC DEF to setup an ATM SVC to NHC KLM, or use an existing PVC, if appropriate.

THE NHRP MESSAGES

This section examines the format and contents of the NHRP messages. Each message consists of a fixed part, a mandatory part, and an extensions part. The fixed part is the same for all messages; the mandatory part is also common to all messages, but its content varies, depend-

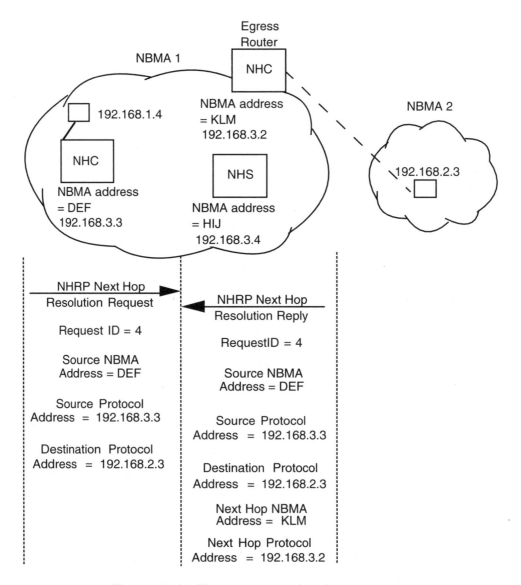

Figure 10–2 The request and reply messages.

ing on the type of message. The extensions part may not be present, and also varies with the message type.

The fixed part of the message is shown in Table 10–1. The function column describes the function of each field.

The mandatory part is shown in Table 10–4. As before, the function column describes the function of each field.

Table 10–1   Fixed Part of the NHRP Message

Name	Function	Size
ar$afn	Defines link layer address being used, based on the Internet address family number published in RFC 1700.	2
ar$pro.type	Protocol type, see Table 10–2 for more information.	2
ar$pro.snap	Used as a SNAP extension when ar$pro.type = 0x0080. SNAP used to code the protocol type.	5
ar$hopcnt	Maximum hop count for an NHRP packet, which represents maximum number of NHSs that can be traversed before the message is discarded.	1
ar$pktsz	Total length of packet, including link layer encapsulation.	2
ar$chksum	IP-type checksum over entire NHRP packet.	2
ar$extoff	Existence and location of NRHP extensions.	2
ar$op.version	Set to 0x01 for use by NHRP.	1
ar$op.type	Type of NHRP packet, see Table 10–3 for more information.	1
ar$shtl	Type and length of NBMA address indicated in ar$afn; example: ar$afn = 8, an E.164 address is coded here.	1
ar$sstl	Same as previous field, except for NBMA subaddress. NBMA may not use a subaddress, in which case, no storage is allocated.	1

Table 10–5 shows the format for the NHRP resolution request message. The request message follows the routed path from the source protocol address to the destination protocol address. The mandatory part of the message was explained earlier, and this table shows the rules for coding the mandatory part for the request message. The Function column of the table explains the functions of each field in the message. The request message may have additional fields called the client information entries (CIEs), which is beyond the scope of this chapter and not needed for this

Table 10–2   Coding for Protocol Type Field

Contents	Meaning
0x0000–0x00FF	Protocols defined by equivalent NLPIDs
0x0100–0x03FF	Reserved for use by the IETF
0x0400–0x04FF	Used by ATM Forum
0x0500–0x05FF	Experimental or local use
0x0600–0xFFFF	Protocol defined by equivalent Ethertypes

**Table 10–3   Coding for NHRP
Packet Type**

Contents	Meaning
1	Next hop resolution request
2	Next hop resolution reply
3	Registration request
4	Registration reply
5	Purge request
6	Purge reply
7	Error indication

discussion. The reader can refer to Section 5.2.0.1 of the NHRP specification if more information is needed.

Table 10–6 shows the format for the NHRP resolution reply message.

PROS AND CONS OF NHRP

The advantage that NHRP has over the conventional methods of IP/ATM internetworking is the ability to by-pass intermediate routers. It also has some deficiencies:

Table 10–4   Format for Mandatory Part (Common Header)

Name	Function	Size
Src Proto Len	Length of source protocol address	1
Dst Proto Len	Length of destination protocol address	1
Flags	Depends on message	2
Request ID	Used to correlate request and reply messages (and any subsequent purge)	4
Source NMBA address	NBMA address of the sender of request message	v
Source NMBA subaddress	NBMA Subaddress of the sender of request message	v
Source protocol address	Address of station sending request message	v
Destination protocol address	Address of station for which the NBMA next hop is requested (the "target" address)	v

Table 10–5   Format for NHRP Next Hop Resolution Request Message

Name	Function	Size
Src Proto Len	Length of source protocol address	1
Dst Proto Len	Length of destination protocol address	1
Q/A/D/U/S bits	Q: 1=sender is a router, 0=sender is a host	2
	A: 1=reply should be an authoritative answer	
	D: Not used	
	U: 1=Used for managing duplicate entries in NHS cache.	
	S: 1=The binding between the source protocol address and the source NBMA information is stable	
Request ID	Used to correlate request and reply messages (and any subsequent purge)	4
MTU	Maximum transmission unit for target station	2
Holding time	Time that client information is considered valid (used for cache management)	2
Source NMBA address	NBMA address of the sender of request message	v
Source NMBA subaddress	NBMA subaddress of the sender of request message	v
Source protocol address	Address of station sending request message	v
Destination protocol address	Address of station for which the NBMA next hop is requested (the "target" address)	v

- Routing information may not be sent across the same path as data. This situation is a result of cut-through routing which can result in a stable routing loop. To handle this problem, the NHS that responded to an NHRP request message must be aware of any topological change could affect the current (cached) topology data. If a problem is detected, the NHS must send to all nodes a message directing them to purge the invalid information.
- It is permissible for an ingress router to receive a datagram and send a resolution request message, but forward the datagram before an NHRP path is established. Each router along the path might do the same thing. This situation is called the domino effect, and scenarios are being developed to handle the problem (but are not completely spelled-out in the specification).

Table 10–6   Format for NHRP Next Hop Resolution Reply Message

Name	Function	Size
Src Proto Len	Length of source protocol address	1
Dst Proto Len	Length of destination protocol address	1
Q/A/B bits	Q: 1=sender is a router, 0=sender is a host (copied from request message A: 1=reply is an authoritative answer D: 1=association between destination and next hop information is stable (route is reliable) U: 1= used for managing duplicate entries in NHS cache. S: Copied from request message	2
NAK code	0=reply is positive, information on binding of internetwork layer and NBMA address has been found	1
Request ID	Used to correlate request and reply messages (and any subsequent purge)	4
MTU	Maximum transmission unit for target station	2
Holding time	Time that client information is considered valid (used for cache management)	2
NH addr T/L	Type and length of next hop NBMA address	1
NH Saddr T/L	Type and length of next hop NBMA subaddress	1
NH Proto len	Length of next hop protocol address	1
Preference	Preference of next hop entry	1
Source NMBA address	NBMA address of the sender of request message	v
Source NMBA subaddress	NBMA subaddress of the sender of request message	v
Source protocol address	Address of station sending request message	v
Destination protocol address	Address of station for which the NBMA next hop is requested (the "target" address)	v
Next hop NBMA address	NBMA address of station in the next hop for traffic bound for the internetwork address specified	v
Next hop NBMA subaddress	NBMA subaddress of station in the next hop for traffic bound for the internetwork address specified	v
Next hop protocol address	Internetwork address of the next hop, which is the destination host if it is directly attached to NBMA subnetwork, otherwise it is the address of the egress router to the destination	v

OTHER NHRP OPERATIONS

This chapter describes the basic NHRP functions. The specification provides more information on:

- PDU forwarding options
- Deployment ideas
- More information on configuration
- Purge operations
- Transit NHSs

SUMMARY

The next hop resolution protocol (NHRP) is responsible for providing a internetwork layer address and its corresponding NBMA subnetwork address for the next hop to a destination station. NHRP is also responsible for finding the egress router from the local NBMA if the destination device is not attached locally to the NBMA network. A number of the NHRP concepts pertain to LANE operations and NHRP employs the client/server model in a manner similar to LANE. The principal difference between LANE and NHRP is that LANE resolves MAC and ATM addresses while NHRP resolves layer 3 and ATM addresses (as well as performing next hop discovery operations).

11

Multiprotocol over ATM (MPOA)

$\mathbf{T}$his chapter explains the operations of Multi-protocol over ATM (MPOA). The discussion revolves around version 1.0 published by the ATM Forum. MPOA has not reached the final ballot. It was approved on a letter ballot, May 29, 1997. This chapter provides the reader with the latest information on MPOA, but be aware that it may change (slightly) as the specification goes through its final balloting.

PURPOSE OF MPOA

In previous chapters, we learned that LAN emulation (LANE) emulates the services of Ethernet, 802.3, and Token Ring LANs through an ATM network. We also learned that LANE allows a subnetwork to be bridged across an ATM/LAN boundary. LANE provides a means for bridging intra-subnet data across an ATM network, but it does not define the operations for inter-subnet traffic that is forwarded through routers, since it uses MAC addresses and not L_3 internetwork addresses.

Advantages of L_3 Operations

L_3 operations provide several advantages over L_2 operations. L_3-based systems are capable of routing datagrams and do not need the broadcast mechanisms of L_2-systems. One reason for this improvement is the fact that L_2 addresses (MAC addresses) are flat addresses and have no hierarchical structure, whereas L_3 addresses (specifically IP and OSI addresses) are structured with a hierarchical syntax. This hierarchical structure is more efficient for route table lookups, since the upper hierarchy values can be examined (for example, network address) without regard to the lower hierarchy structures (for example, a node address) until the datagram reaches the network node (router) to which the end station is attached. Then, the lower-hierarchy address can be examined to determine the final destination end-node.

In addition, L_3 protocols contain a field in the L_3 header called either the type of service (TOS) or quality of service (QOS). This field can be used by the network to tailor the service to the user, a capability that is becoming increasingly important in multiserve environments.

INTRA-SUBNET AND INTER-SUBNET OPERATIONS

With these ideas in mind, let us return to the concepts of intra-subnet operations and inter-subnet operations shown in Figures 11–1 and 11–2. In Figure 11–1, an emulated LAN (ELAN) is connected through bridges or edge devices by ATM LANE. The network and subnetwork address for the bridges and hosts is 192.168.1. All units in this ELAN are identified by the same IP subnet address (class C addresses in

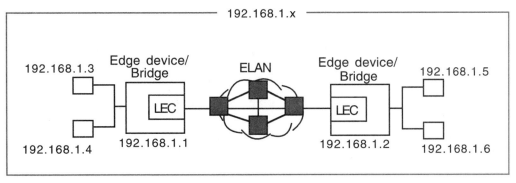

where:

■ = ATM switch

Figure 11–1   Bridging intra-subnet traffic across an ATM network.

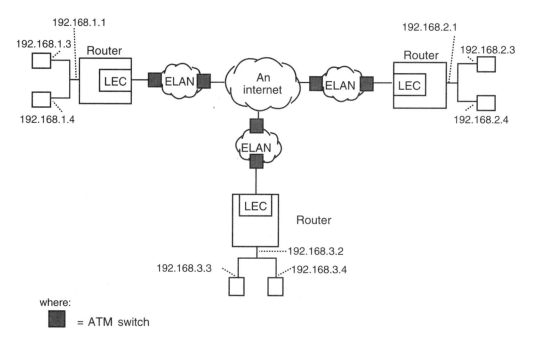

where:

■ = ATM switch

Figure 11–2   Routing inter-subnetwork traffic across ATM and Internet networks.

this example). Thus, each host number is based on this subnet address and intra-subnet operations are bridged across the ATM/LAN boundary. Indeed, the only reason that the bridges might be given an IP address is for purposes of management, but a bridge does not need a L_3 address for its ongoing bridging operations.

Figure 11–2 shows an example of inter-subnetwork operations. In this scenario, we have three subnetworks, identified as 192.168.1, 192.168.2, and 192.168.3, that are connected through ELANs into an internet. Conventional LANE operations will not work in this environment, because L_3 addresses are needed to route the traffic beyond the LANs.

Recall from Chapter 10 that the Next Hop Resolution Protocol (NHRP) allows intermediate routers to be bypassed, and in Figure 11–2, the routers in the internet may be bypassed if a shortcut (a VCC) exists between two of these subnetworks. However, NHRP does not define how to discover addresses beyond its NBMA and relies on an egress router in the NBMA to find the address through conventional route discovery protocols. Furthermore, NHRP assumes the routers involved in its operations perform internetwork layer route calculations.

MPOA goes several steps further than LANE and NHRP. First, it incorporates the operations of LANE and NHRP, thus retaining the advantages of bridging, but it also supports the use of internetwork layer communications (L_3 routing). It continues to use ATM VCCs for the transfer of traffic and has schemes for bypassing routers. At the same time, inter-subnet operations are supported (for unicast traffic). Furthermore, MPOA defines operations that enable an edge device to perform internetwork layer datagram *forwarding* operations without having to perform *route calculations*. This feature reduces the complexity and expense of these machines.

As a result of this extension, MPOA devices define shortcut interfaces for shortcut VCCs, as shown in Figure 11–3. Traffic coming from a bridge connected to an ELAN can be sent to another ELAN through a LEC service interface or to a shortcut VCC through a shortcut interface. Traffic coming from a shortcut VCC can be relayed to a local ELAN, or to another shortcut VCC.

Figure 11–4 illustrates the MPOA approach. Additional components are added to the system, and one is called the MPOA client (MPC). The MPC, say the MPC at subnet 192.168.1, is able to determine that a better path exists between subnets 192.168.1 and 192.168.3. The path is an ATM VCC and is used to provide the shortcut between the two systems.

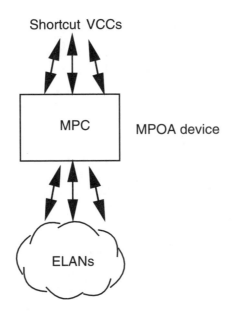

Figure 11–3   Example of the MPOA device interfaces.

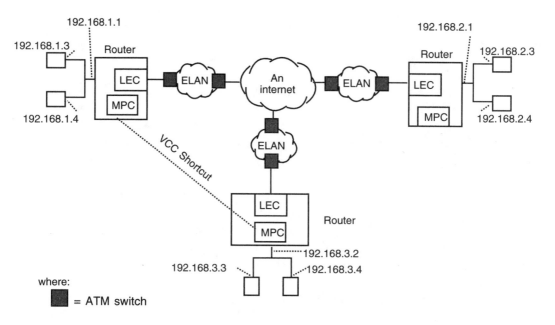

Figure 11–4   The VCC shortcut.

The MPOA resolution request protocol is used to obtain the information about the shortcut and is discussed shortly.

In summary, the principal objective of MPOA is to support the transfer of inter-subnet unicast traffic in a LANE environment. MPOA allows the inter-subnetwork traffic based on layer 3 protocol communications to occur over ATM virtual channel connections (VCCs) without requiring routers in the data path. The goal of MPOA is to combine bridging and routing with ATM in a situation where diverse protocols and network topologies exist.

The job of MPOA is to provide this operation to allow the overlaying of layer 3 protocols (also called internetwork layer protocols) on ATM. MPOA is designed to use both routing and bridging information to locate the optimal route through the ATM backbone.

Virtual Routing

MPOA supports the concept of virtual routing, which is the separation of internetwork layer route calculation and forwarding. The idea behind virtual routing is to enhance the manageability of internetworking by decreasing the number of devices that are configured to perform route calculation. In so doing, virtual routing increases scalability by reducing the number of devices that participate in the inter-network layer route calculations. The edge device cited above is one such example.

MPOA REQUIREMENTS

MPOA is based on the implementation of the ATM Forum's signaling protocol that supports Releases UNI 3.0, UNI 3.1, or UNI 4.0. It requires the use of LANE Version 2.0. It also requires the use of NHRP.

MPOA CACHE

Ingress Cache

The overall operations of MPOA are managed by cache entries. If an incoming datagram's protocol is "enabled"—this means it is eligible for shortcut routing—and the MPC examines its ingress cache for a match of the datagram's internetwork destination address and a like entry in the ingress cache. The ingress cache contents are:

- *Key:* MPS control ATM address
- *Key:* Internetwork layer destination address
- *Contents:*
  - Destination ATM address or a VCC
  - Encapsulation information
  - Other (timers, flow counts, etc.)

Therefore, the ingress cache contains the necessary information to resolve the L_3 destination address to an ATM address of VCC.

In summary, ingress cache deals with traffic entering the MPOA system and is used to detect flows that can use a shortcut and an appropriate shortcut VCC.

Egress Cache

Egress cache is used to determine how L_3 datagrams coming from a shortcut are to be encapsulated and forwarded.

For the traffic coming on a shortcut, the egress MPC is searched for a hit on a source/destination ATM address pair and the internetwork layer destination address. The egress cache contents are:

- *Key:* Internetwork layer destination address
- *Key:* ATM source/destination address
- *Key:* Optional tag
- *Contents:*
  - LEC identifier
  - DLC header
  - Other (holding time, etc.)

Therefore, the egress cache contains the necessary information to resolve the ATM and L_3 addresses to an LEC.

MPOA CLIENTS AND SERVERS

Like many protocols in the ATM internetworking families, MPOA uses the client-server architecture. The client is called the MPOA client (MPC) and the server is called the MPOA server (MPS). These clients and servers are connected through an ELAN. The relationship of MPC and MPS are shown in Figure 11–5. MPOA also describes the edge device cited earlier, which supports connections to legacy LANs. The edge devices support L_3 forwarding but do not have to perform L_3 route discovery (OSPF, RIP, etc.).

In this section, a description is provided of the egress/ingress MPSs and MPCs. It will be helpful to refer to Figure 11–6 during this discussion.

The datagram is received by an ingress MPC. A default path entails the bridging of the traffic through a LANE to a router (through MPC 1). Eventually, it leaves the system via MPC 2's LEC interface.

However, if the datagram is associated with a shortcut flow, the ingress MPC removes the DLL encapsulation and sends the datagram

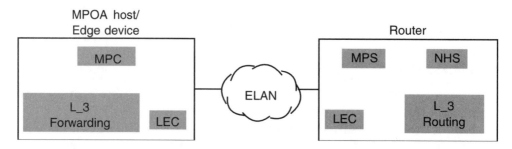

Figure 11–5   MPOA components.

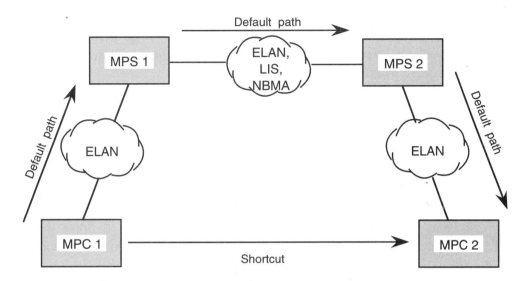

Figure 11–6   Shortcuts and default paths.

onto the ATM shortcut (perhaps adding tagging information, discussed later).

If there is no shortcut flow detected, each datagram is counted (a count is accumulated relative to a destination L_3 address). When the count reaches a threshold, the ingress MPC1 must send an MPOA resolution request message to MPS1. The purpose of this message is to obtain the downstream ATM address for the shortcut—in this example, MPC2. This process is illustrated on the left side of Figure 11–6. Now, we can move forward to an analysis of the roles of the MPCs and MPSs and also examine the other aspects of Figure 11–6.

The MPC

The principal function of the MPC is to perform internetwork layer forwarding of traffic. But it is not required to run the internetwork layer routing protocols. The MPC acts as a source and sink for the internetwork shortcuts. The MPC must support one or more L_3 addresses and an ATM address in this fashion:

- L_3 address of MPC (and an associated ATM address) represents the address of the node having the MPC
- L_3 addresses (and an associated ATM address) that are reachable through the node (when the node is an edge device or a router). The L_3 addresses are typically IP subnet addresses.

The MPC performs different functions in its ingress role (recall that ingress is the point where inbound data flow enters the MPOA system) and its egress role (also recall that egress is the point where outbound data flow exits the MPOA system).

For the ingress operation, the MPC must detect traffic that is being forwarded over an ELAN to a router that contains an MPS. Its job is to recognize a flow that could benefit from a shortcut that bypasses the ongoing routed path. To support this operation, it sends an MPOA resolution request to the ingress MPS to establish a shortcut to the desired destination. Upon obtaining this information, the MPC stores this information, sets up the shortcut VCC, and forwards the traffic over the shortcut to the destination.

As the traffic flows into the MPC, the frames are checked to determine if the destination MAC address is for an MPS. If so, and detection is enabled for the protocol (it is subject to a shortcut), the MPC then examines the internetwork destination address in the datagram header and looks up the corresponding entry in the ingress cache. The key values in the ingress cache are <MPS ATM address, Internetwork layer address>. If this is a hit, and a valid shortcut is defined in the ingress cache for this traffic, the traffic is sent to the ingress shortcut service interface. If it is not a valid shortcut, it is sent onto an outbound LEC service interface.

For the egress operation, the MPC is tasked with forwarding traffic to its local users. It performs this operation by receiving traffic from other MPCs. Upon receiving frames received over a shortcut, the MPC must add the appropriate data link layer (DLL) encapsulation operations and forward this traffic to the higher layers. These higher layers may be an upper-layer internal protocol family stack or it may be a bridge port. The DLL encapsulation must be provided to the egress MPC by its egress MPS. This information must be stored at MPC (in the call MPC egress cache). The egress MPC may also send the traffic onto one of its ELAN interfaces.

The egress MPC is also responsible for responding to cache imposition request messages sent by an egress MPS. The message is sent to the egress MPC to determine if this node has the required resources to support a new VCC and to maintain the cache entry. The message also provides encapsulation information that will be needed by the egress MPC when it encapsulates outbound traffic.

The role of the ingress MPOA server (MPS) to answer MPOA queries from local MPCs (NHS may be co-located in the router that houses the MPC). It also is responsible for providing DLL encapsulation information to egress MPCs. The MPS also provides DLL encapsulation information to egress MPCs. It is also responsible for converting between MPOA requests and replies as well as NHRP requests and replies.

If the ingress MPS cannot answer to the MPOA resolution request (from the local MPC) because the target address is not local, then it simply resends ("re-originates" is the term used in the specification) the message through the routed path to the local NHRP next hop server (NHA). This message is changed slightly: The L_3 source protocol address field is filled in with the reoriginating ingress MPS so that a reply is returned to it and not the actual originator. However, the MPC's ATM address remains as the source NBMA address; otherwise, a correlation cannot be made to the actual originator. When the ingress MPS receives a reply to its reoriginated message, it returns an MPOA resolution reply to the ingress MPC.

The egress MPS receives NHRP resolution requests targeted for a local MPC (in this example, the egress MPS is the NHRP authoritative server for that MPC). Based on the contents in the NHRP resolution request message, this egress MPS constructs an MPOA cache imposition request and sends this message to the egress MPC. The function of this message was described in the description of the role of the egress MPC.

THE USE OF TAGS

The egress cache may contain a tag. A tag is used to encapsulate data that is sent over a shortcut. An egress cache is used to find an appropriate shortcut (if one exists). When outbound packets are received, the egress MPC looks for a hit on ATM address and destination internetwork layer address. Optionally, a tag can be stored for the cache entry, and the hit can be made on the tag. This concept is called by various names in the industry—a common descriptor is tag switching. The goal of tag switching is to avoid the slow lookups with conventional L_3 routing tables.

MPOA INFORMATION FLOWS

MPOA operations entail several information flows that are categorized as MPOA control flows and MPOA data flows. All control and data flows operate over ATM VCs using LLC/SNAP encapsulation, in accordance with RFC 1483. The control flows are further defined as (1) configuration flows, (2) MPC/MPS control flows, (3) MPS/MPS control flows, and (4) MPC-MPC control flows. The configuration flows use the conventional LANE formats, and the LANE LECS. The MPOA data flows are categorized as MPC-MPC data flows and MPC-NHC data flows. Examples of these flows are provided in Figure 11–7.

Configuration flows are used by MPSs and MPCs to communicate with the LAN emulation configuration server (LECS) to receive configuration information in accordance with the LANE specification.

MPC/MPS control flows are used between an edge device or MPOA host and a router for MPC cache management. It also allows the ingress MPC to obtain shortcut information. In addition, the MPS can take the

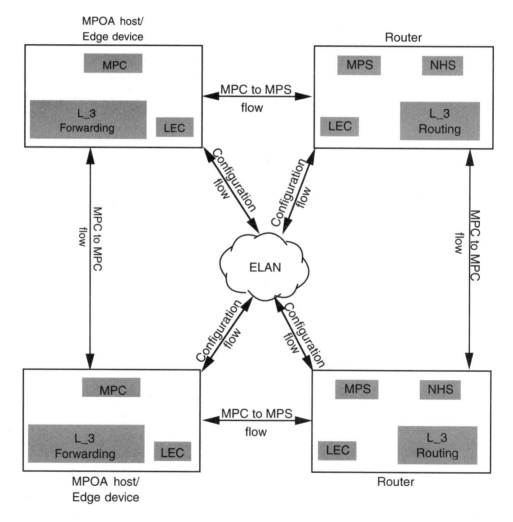

Figure 11–7   MPOA flows.

action by sending a trigger message to the MPC. Also the egress MPS gives the egress MPC egress cache information with a cache imposition reply message. These messages are discussed later.

The MPS-MPS control flows are exchanged between two routers in accordance with ongoing routing protocols and NHRP.

The MPC-MPC control flows are used by an egress MPC to send a purge to an ingress MPC if it received misdirected packets from that MPC.

Finally, the MPOA data flows (MPC-MPC and MPC-NHC) are used for the transfer of traffic between MPCs and between an MPC and an NHC. MPC-MPC data flows are used for shortcut VCCs, and MPC-NHC data flows are used to send unicast data to an MPC.

MAJOR MPOA OPERATIONS

MPOA is responsible for five major operations:

1. *Configuration:* This operation obtains configuration information from the ELAN LECS.
2. *Discovery:* MPCs and MPSs dynamically learn of each other's existence. MPCs and MPSs discover each other by using minor additions to the LANE LE_ARP protocol. These messages carry the MPOA device type (MPC or MPS) and its ATM Address
3. *Target Resolution:* This operation uses a modified NHRP Resolution Request message MPCs to resolve the ATM Address for the end points of a shortcut. Also, the mapping of a target to an egress ATM address is provided, as well as an optional tag (discussed later) and a set of parameters used to set up a shortcut VCC to forward traffic across subnet boundaries.
4. *Connection Management:* This operation controls the ongoing management of VCCs transfer control information and data.
5. *Data Transfer:* This operation is responsible forwarding of internetwork layer traffic across a shortcut.

EXAMPLES OF MPOA OPERATIONS

This section provides three examples of MPOA operations with the goal of piecing together the concepts covered thus far in this chapter. The focus in the examples will be how the MPC in a machine discovers a data

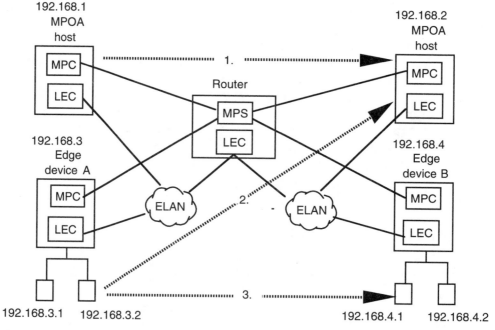

where:
    Shortcut 1: MPOA host-to-MPOA host.
    Shortcut 2: Edge device-to-MPOA host.
    Shortcut 3: Edge device-to-Edge device.

Figure 11–8   Three shortcut examples.

flow that can benefit from a shortcut and how the shortcut is used. The three examples are listed here and depicted in Figure 11–8 with the dashed lines. This figure will also be used for each of our examples:

- Shortcut 1: MPOA host-to-MPOA host
- Shortcut 2: Edge device-to-MPOA host
- Shortcut 3: Edge device-to-edge device

MPOA Host-to-MPOA Host

Figure 11–9 shows how a shortcut is established between two MPOA hosts. One host resides on subnet 192.168.1 and the other host resides on subnet 192.168.2. Before the shortcut is established, MPOA host 192.168.1 forwards its traffic in a LANE frame to a router through a LANE data direct VCC. This operation is shown in Figure 11–9a with the notation ELAN above the arrow (the direction of the arrow symbol-

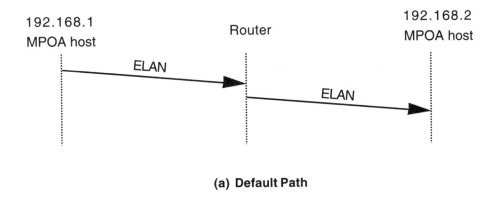

(a) Default Path

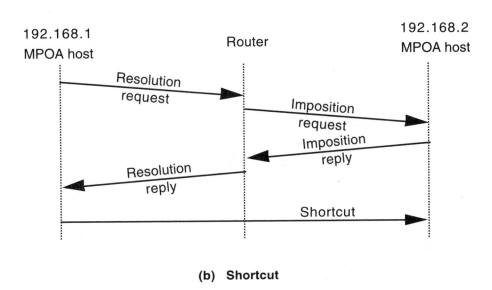

(b) Shortcut

Figure 11–9   Shortcut example 1: MPOA host—MPOA host.

izes the flow of the traffic). The router receives the traffic but must use a different data direct VCC to forward the LANE frame to MPOA host 192.168.2.

The sending MPOA host has been examining the headers in this flow, and it is able to detect the internetwork layer address of the receiving MPOA host. Based on this detection, it sends an MPOA resolution request message to the MPS to obtain an ATM address. This message is sent to the router. In effect, the router uses the information in the MPOA resolution request message to construct and send an MPOA cache imposition request message to MPOA host 192.168.2. This message will ask host 192.168.2 to provide an egress cache entry.

This host then creates an MPOA cache imposition reply that indicates that it will accept the shortcut. As shown in Figure 11–9b, this reply is sent back to the router, which translates this message into an MPOA resolution reply. It then sends this reply to the originating host. The reply contains the ATM address of MPOA host of 192.168.2. Upon receiving the MPOA resolution reply message, the MPOA host 192.168.1 updates its ingress cache and establishes the shortcut to the other MPOA host.

Now that these important housekeeping functions have been completed, MPOA host 192.168.1 sends its internetwork layer traffic (typically IP datagrams) using the appropriate encapsulation procedures defined for the shortcut. The identification of the appropriate VCC for this shortcut is contained in the ingress cache entry.

H2 Edge Device-to-MPOA host

Figure 11–10 shows the operations for the development of a shortcut between an edge device and an MPOA host. For this example, traffic emanates from host 192.168.3.2 and is to be forwarded to the MPOA host 192.168.2. The operations in this example are the same as in the previous example. The only addition is the depiction of traffic flowing from host 192.168.3.2 to its edge device (labeled edge device A). Just as in the previous example, MPOA resolution operations occur between the edge device and the router and cache imposition operations occur between the router and the MPOA host. The end result is still the same, the agreement on a shortcut with its appropriate VCC and the subsequent use of that shortcut.

Edge Device-to-Edge Device

Finally, Figure 11–11 shows the use of a shortcut to deliver traffic between two edge devices (edge device A and edge device B) and the subsequent traffic to the hosts attached the devices. The ongoing operations entailing MPOA resolution and cache imposition messages are identical to the previous examples.

ROLES OF MPS AND MPC IN MORE DETAIL

This section provides a more detailed look at the roles of the MPS and MPC. I have included in Figure 11–12 the MPC data path processing logical block diagram, which is derived from the MPOA ATM Forum BTD-MPOA-MPOA-01.16 specification.

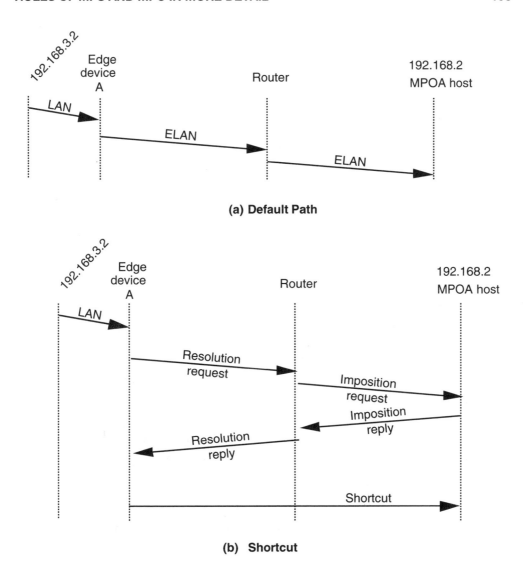

Figure 11–10   Shortcut example 2: Edge device—MPOA host.

An ingress MPC discovers the MAC addresses of MPSs attached to its ELANs from the device type type-length-values (TLVs) in LANE LE_ARP responses. The MPC performs flow detection, based on the L_3 destination address, on packets destined for the MAC addresses.

Default forwarding takes place through routers, and this route will remain unless a shortcut is discovered. When the MPC becomes cognizant of a traffic flow that might benefit from a shortcut, the ingress MPC must determine the ATM address associated with the egress device. To obtain the ATM address for a shortcut, the ingress MPC sends

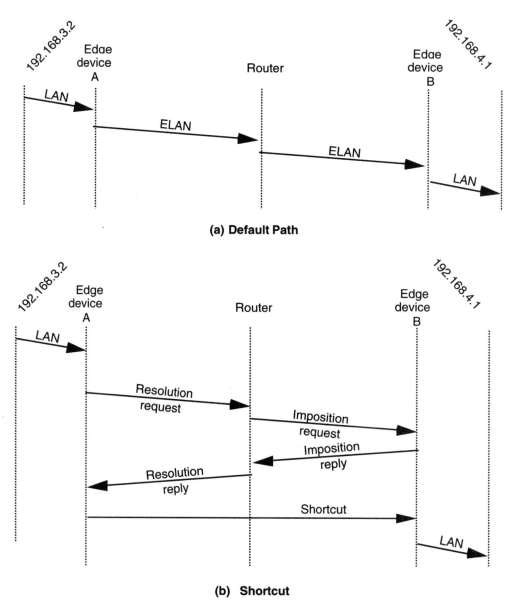

(a) Default Path

(b) Shortcut

Figure 11–11   Shortcut example 3: Edge device — Edge device.

an MPOA resolution request packet to the appropriate ingress MPS. When this MPS is able to resolve the MPOA resolution request, a reply is returned to the ingress MPC.

The ingress MPS processes MPOA resolution requests sent by local MPCs. The ingress MPS is allowed to respond to the request if the destination is local. If the address in non-local, the MPS sends (reoriginates) the

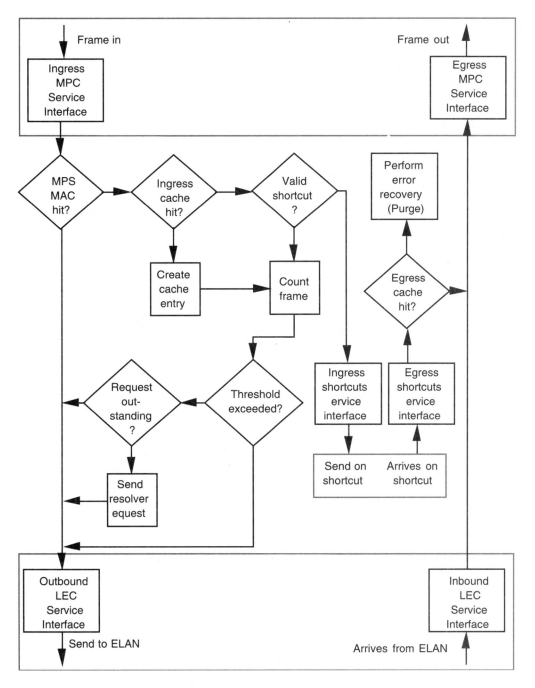

Figure 11–12   The logic flow for MPOA.

request through the routed path. The ingress MPS uses its internetwork layer address as the source protocol address in this request. This operation provides assurance that the reply is returned to the originating MPS.

The MPS copies all other fields from the resolution request packet. The MPC's data ATM address is used as the source NBMA. The MPS generates a new Request ID for the reoriginated request. On receiving a reply to this reoriginated request, the ingress MPS sets the Request ID field and source protocol address to the original values and returns an MPOA resolution reply to the ingress MPC.

When an resolution request packet targeted for a local MPC arrives at the egress MPS serving that MPC, the egress MPS constructs an MPOA Cache Imposition Request, which is sent to the egress MPC.

The Cache Imposition Request provides encapsulation and state maintenance information needed by the egress MPC, and the MPOA Cache Imposition Reply provides status, address, and ingress tagging information used by the egress MPS to formulate the NHRP resolution reply packet.

After receiving the Cache Imposition Reply packet from the egress MPC, the egress MPS sends an resolution reply packet toward the request originator.

The egress MPC must send an Cache Imposition Reply packet for every Cache Imposition request. To formulate the reply, the MPC decides if it has the resources needed to maintain the cache entry and support a new VCC. If the Cache Imposition is an update of an existing egress cache entry, the resources should be available. If the MPC cannot accept either the cache entry or the potential VCC, it sets the appropriate error status and returns the MPOA Cache Imposition Reply to the MPS. Otherwise, the MPC inserts an ATM address and sends the Cache Imposition Reply to the egress MPS.

The main incentive for including a tag is to solve the egress cache conflict. But, tags can also be used to improve the egress cache lookup. This improvement can be achieved by providing an index into the egress cache as the tag. When the tag is an index into the cache, the cache search is reduced to a direct cache lookup.

THE MPOA PROTOCOL DATA UNITS (PDUs) FORMATS

Figure 11–13 shows the encapsulation formats for LLC and tagged traffic. There is little information to add here; these formats have been covered extensively in Chapters 2 and 6.

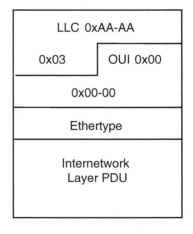

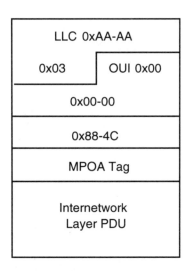

(a) RFC 1483 LLC Encapsulation   **(b) Tagged Encapsulation**

Figure 11–13   Encapsulation conventions.

FORMAT AND SYNTAX FOR THE MPOA MESSAGES

Most of the rules for coding the MPOA messages are derived from NHRP. Tables 11–1, 11–2, and 11–3 explain the fixed part and the resolution request and response messages.

Table 11–1   Fixed Part of the MPOA Message

Name	Function	Size
ar$afn	Defines link layer address being used	2
ar$pro.type	Protocol type, see Table 10-2 for more information	2
ar$pro.snap	Used as a SNAP extension when ar$pro.type=0x0080	5
ar$hopcnt	Maximum hop count for an NHRP packet	1
ar$pktsz	Total length of packet, including link layer encapsulation	2
ar$chksum	IP-type checksum over entire NHRP packet	2
ar$extoff	Existence and location of NRHP extensions	2
ar$op.version	Set to 0x01 for version 1	1
ar$op.type	Type of MPOA message (e.g., 134=MPOA Resolution Request, 135=MPOA Resolution Reply	
ar$shtl	Type and length of ATM address indicated in ar$afn; example: ar$afn=8, an E.164 address is coded here	1
ar$sstl	Same as previous field, except for ATM subaddress	1

Table 11–2   Format for MPOA Resolution Request Message

Name	Function	Size
Flags (NRHP)	Not used	2
Source NMBA address	ATM address of the ingress MPC from which interwork layer datagrams will be sent	v
Source NMBA subaddress	ATM subaddress of the ingress MPC from which interwork layer datagrams will be sent	v
Source protocol address	Address of MPC sending request message (optional)	v
Destination protocol address	Address of the final destination to which datagrams will be sent	v

Note: The header preceding these fields is based on the NHRP fixed header.

Several other messages are used, of course, such as the imposition requests and replies. The reader should refer to the details of the specifications, if more information is needed.

OTHER MPOA OPERATIONS

We have learned about the basic architecture and operations of MPOA. But, we have only touched the surface. The complete specification is 101 pages in length (excluding Annex C, NBMA). The interested reader might wish to obtain the specification to learn about these other MPOA features:

Table 11–3   Format for MPOA Resolution Reply Message

Name	Function	Size
Flags (NRHP)	Not used	2
Source NMBA address	ATM address of the ingress MPC from which interwork layer datagrams will be sent	v
Source NMBA subaddress	ATM subaddress of the ingress MPC from which interwork layer datagrams will be sent	v
Source protocol address	Copied from corresponding MPOA request message	v
Destination protocol address	Address of the final destination to which datagrams will be sent	v

Note: The header preceding these fields is based on the NHRP fixed header.

- Configuration operations
- Registration operations
- Cache management in more detail
- Connection management and the use of UNI signaling
- Design considerations

SUMMARY

We have learned that MPOA builds on the services offered by LANE and NHRP. Its additional services allow for inter-subnet operations and retains the advantages of both L_2 bridging and L_3 routing. In addition, MPOA provides a means to: (1) bypass intermediate routers by employing a bypass ATM virtual circuit, (2) employ the use of tags to enhance cache lookup, and (3) provide a means for devices to perform internetwork layer forwarding operations without incurring the overhead of performing route calculations for this traffic.

Appendix A

Basics of Internetworking

This Appendix provides an introduction to internetworking. The topics covered are (1) how internetworking came about; (2) route discovery operations (3) connection-oriented and connectionless networks, and (4) bridges, routers, and gateways.

INTERNETWORKING CONFIGURATION

Figure A–1 shows the relationship of subnetworks and routers (internetworking units) to layered protocols. In this figure, it is assumed that the user application in host A sends traffic to an application layer protocol in host B, such as a file. The file transfer software performs a variety of functions and appends a file transfer header to the user data. In many systems, the operations at host B are known as *server* operations and the operations at host A are known as *client* operations.

As indicated with the arrows going down in the protocol stack at host A, this data is passed to the transport layer protocol (the data is called a protocol data unit [PDU]). This layer, often implemented with the Transmission Control Protocol (TCP), performs a variety of operations and adds a header to the PDU passed to it. The unit of data is now

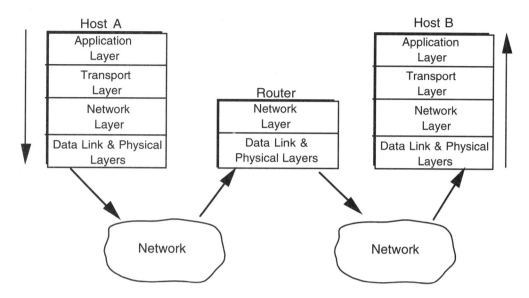

Figure A–1   Layers in an internetworking system.

called a *segment*. The PDU from the upper layers is considered to be data to the transport layer.

Next, the transport layer passes the segment to the network layer, also called the Internet Protocol (IP) layer, which again performs specific services and appends a header. This unit (now called a datagram in Internet terms) is passed down to the lower layers. Here, the data link layer adds its header as well as a trailer, and the data unit (now called a *frame*) is launched into the network by the physical layer. Of course, if host B sends data to host A, the process is reversed and the direction of the arrows is changed.

The host computers are unaware of what goes on inside the network. The network manager is free to manipulate and manage the PDU in any manner necessary.

The router receives the traffic and makes routing decisions based on the addresses provided by the host computer.

The destination (host B) eventually receives the traffic at its lower layers and reverses the process that transpired at host A. That is to say, it decapsulates the headers by stripping them off in the appropriate layer. The header is used by the layer to determine the actions it is to take; the header governs the layer's operations.

EVOLUTION TO INTERNETWORKING

In the early days of internetworking, and especially during the pioneering days of the development of the Internet and packet switching, designers were wrestling with the problem of interfacing different types of host computers (IBM, UNIVAC, Telex terminals) into one network (which was dubbed a backbone network, since it connected these machines together).

The problem was twofold: how to connect the computers with the network nodes (the packet switches) and how to connect the computers to each other, through the network.

For the first problem (we discuss the second problem later), it was decided to build an interface at these network switches that would allow the hosts to connect to the network and send their data to the intended destination. So, the switches would act as a "gateway" into and out of the network (see Figure A–2).

These switches also had to communicate with each other and inform each other about their readiness to accept traffic (or not accept traffic) from each other. That is, they needed a protocol to govern their operations with each other. This protocol became known as a "gateway protocol" in some circles. As the term proliferated, it became associated with the procedures that entailed the exchange of routing information between the switches, as well as between the switches and the hosts.

CONNECTING NETWORKS TOGETHER (INTERNETWORKING)

Due to the many sites in an enterprise (company, government agency, etc.) that needed to communicate with each other, it became necessary to connect existing networks together. As these connections grew, so did the problems associated with a larger (and more complex) system (see Figure A–3).

One of the problems was being able to determine how hosts could be reached through their respective regional networks. Another problem has being able to determine if a switch was capable of relaying traffic to the host; that is, if the switch was "up." In most systems, it was determined that the evolving data network should be able to find a host, find its respective network, and if necessary, divert traffic around a faulty switch or network to reach the host.

In other words, a mechanism should exist that allowed the discovery of a route to the host through switches and networks that were capable of

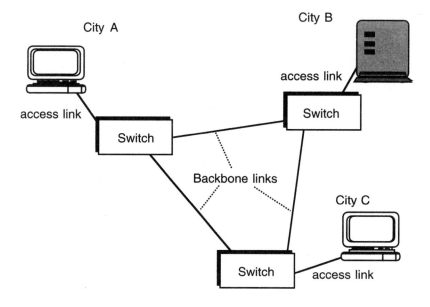

(a) In the early stages of internetworking

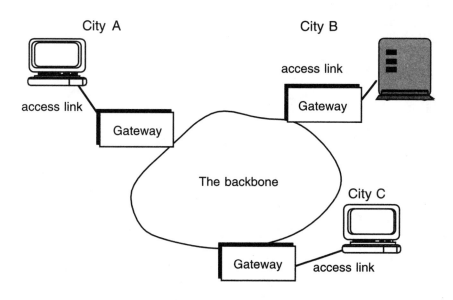

(b) As things evolved . . .

Figure A–2 Evolution of some internetworking terms.

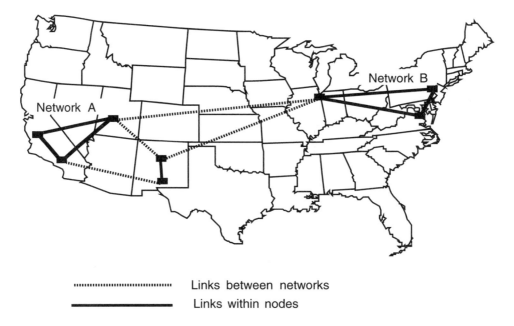

··	Links between networks
────────────────	Links within nodes

Figure A–3   Connecting the networks.

supporting the route. This process entailed the exchange of information among the switches and hosts to keep each other aware of their existence and readiness to accept traffic.

As stated earlier, for lack of a better term, the industry called this overall process a "gateway protocol." Other terms are used today, such as route discovery or routing exchange, but the term gateway protocol is still used.

ROUTE DISCOVERY

The industry has developed several tools for route discovery. They can be classified as a distance, vector (more commonly called minimum hop) or link state metric protocol (see Figure A–4). The distance, vector protocol is based on the idea that it makes the best sense to transmit the traffic through the fewest number of networks and switches (hops). In the past, network designers held that this approach led to the most efficient route through an internet, and perhaps more to the point, it was easy to implement. The fewest hops approach could be debated, but we will confine ourselves to how the approach works, rather than its relative merits. The term distance = a hop count (also called the path length, ob-

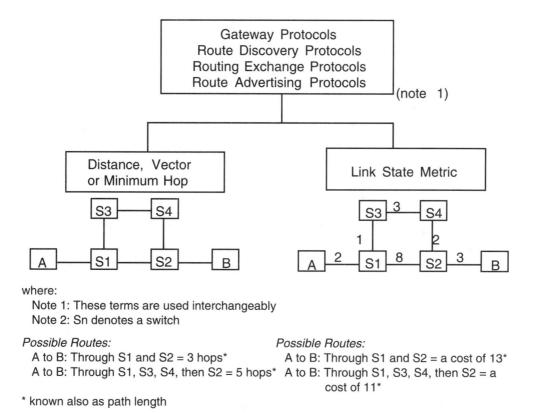

where:
  Note 1: These terms are used interchangeably
  Note 2: Sn denotes a switch

Possible Routes: *Possible Routes:*
  A to B: Through S1 and S2 = 3 hops*   A to B: Through S1 and S2 = a cost of 13*
  A to B: Through S1, S3, S4, then S2 = 5 hops* A to B: Through S1, S3, S4, then S2 = a
                                                                       cost of 11*

* known also as path length

Figure A–4   Typical ways of finding and maintaining a route.

viously a misnomer, since the chosen path has nothing to do with the
length of the path); the term vector = a destination address.

The link state metric protocol is based on a number of criteria called
type of service factors (TOS). The OSI Model uses the term quality of service factors (QOS). These factors are defined by the network administra-
tors and users and may include criteria such as delay, throughput, and
security needs. Each link is assigned a value (metric), which could represent delay, throughput, or any factor that is important to the network administration. A smaller value represents a better service. The chosen
path from the source to the destination is the individual link values that
sum to the smallest total.

The path through an internet is chosen based on the ability of the
switches and networks to meet a required service. This technique is also
called *link state routing*, because the TOS values are applied to each communication link in the internet. It is also called shortest path first (SPF),

once again the term "shortest" does not mean the shortest distance, but the smallest total of the link state metrics.

Figure A–4 shows examples of the two techniques and some possible routes for traffic sent from host A to host B. For the minimum hop protocol, the best path is from host A→S1→S2→host B, because it goes through the fewest number of hops. For the link state metric protocol, the best path is from host A→S1→S3→S4→S2→host B. The link between S1 and S2 precludes using this link because of the high cost (8). This cost could be a result of a low-speed link, or a link that is experiencing degraded throughput.

CONNECTIONLESS AND CONNECTION-ORIENTED PROTOCOLS

The concept of connectionless and connection-oriented operations is fundamental to any communications protocol. See Tables A–1 and A–2. It is essential that the reader has a clear understanding of their features.

The connection-oriented service requires a three-way agreement between the two end users and the service provider (for instance, the network). It also allows the communicating parties to negotiate certain options and quality of service (QOS) functions. During the connection establishment, all three parties store information about each other, such as addresses and QOS features, in tables. Once data transfer begins, the PDUs need not carry much overhead protocol control information (PCI). All that is needed is an abbreviated identifier to allow the parties to access the tables to determine the route and its associated QOS. Since the session can be negotiated, the communicating parties need not have prior knowledge of all the characteristics of each other. If a requested service cannot be provided, any of the parties can negotiate the service to a lower level or reject the connection request.

The connection-oriented service may or may not provide for the acknowledgment of all data units. Also, this approach entails fixed routing within the network since the PDUs do not contain sufficient address information to permit dynamic (on-the-spot) routing decisions. This route is also called a virtual connection (VC).

Table A–1   Connection-Oriented Networks

- Connection mapped through network
- Abbreviated addressing (a virtual circuit ID)
- Usually fixed routing between/within network(s)
- Accountability of traffic may or may not be provided

Table A–2   Connectionless Service

- Limited or no end-to-end mapping of connection
- Full addressing in each protocol data unit (PDU)
- Can use alternate routing
- Accountability of traffic may or may not be provided

Connectionless protocols do not create a connection or virtual circuit. Since no information is kept about the users of this approach, each PDU must have complete addressing information, which can result in large headers for *each* PDU. On the other hand, full addressing permits dynamic routing, since the switches do not have any "preconceived" rules for the route (no virtual circuit mapping tables). Finally, most connectionless protocols do not offer acknowledgment or sequencing services.

Figure A–5 illustrates the concepts of connection-oriented and connectionless systems. As just stated, in order for machines to communicate through a connection-oriented network, they must go through a handshake, also called a connection establishment. During this process, the switches may negotiate the services that are to be used during the session. Once the connection is established, data are exchanged in consonance with the negotiations that occurred during the connection-establishment phase.

The connection-oriented network provides a substantial amount of care for the signaling PDUs that set up the connection. The procedure requires an acknowledgment from the network and responding user that the connection is established; otherwise, the requesting machine must be informed as to why the connection request was not successful. The network must also maintain an awareness of the connection. Flow control (i.e., making certain that all the data arrives correctly, in order, and does not saturate the user computers in the various parts of the network) is also required of most connection oriented networks.

As we just learned, the connectionless (also called *datagram*) network goes directly to the data transfer mode, followed later by the idle condition. The major difference between this network and the connection-oriented network is the absence of the connection establishment and release phases. Moreover, a connectionless network has no end-to-end acknowledgments, flow control, or error recovery.

It should be noted that a network may use a mixture of connection-oriented and connectionless techniques. Indeed, some organizations (that must transfer data between networks) use X.25 or Frame Relay as the connection-oriented, user-to-network interface and then implement a connectionless protocol within the network.

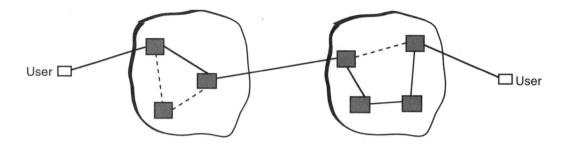

- - - - - -   Dashed line means switch/router did not
              participate in the call connection procedure

▨   Switch/router with solid lines map source & destination
    addresses to a virtual circuit number

(a) Connection-Oriented Procedure

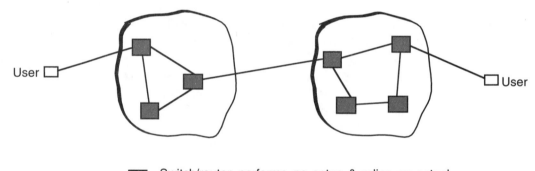

▨   Switch/router performs no setup & relies on actual
    addresses for identifying traffic

(b) Connectionless Procedure

Figure A–5   Connection-oriented and connectionless networks.

INTERFACES

Network services are typically provided at three interfaces: (1) the
interface between the user and the network; (2) the interface between
networks; and less frequently, (3) the interface within a network. These
interfaces are shown in Figure A–6, as well as the common terms associated with the interfaces. They are:

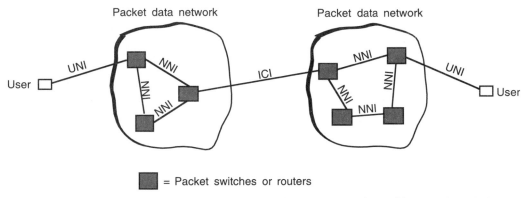

Note 1: The initial NNI is also used as: (a) network-network interface, (b) network-node interface, and may also identify the interface between networks (the ICI in this figure).

where:
  UNI = User-network interface
  NNI = Node-node interface
  ICI   = Intercarrier interface

Figure A–6   Where network services are provided.

- The user-network interface (UNI)
- The node-node interface (NNI) (see note 1 for Figure A–6)
- The intercarrier interface (ICI) (see note 1 for Figure A–6)

The initial thrust of network services was on the interface between the user and the network (the UNI). However, the intercarrier interface is also quite important, because many organizations that need to communicate with each other are connected through different networks. Historically, the operations within a network have been proprietary and specific to a vendor's implementation. This situation is changing, although most internal operations still remain proprietary and are not standardized.

GATEWAYS, BRIDGES, AND ROUTERS

Networks were originally conceived to be fairly small systems consisting of a relatively few machines. As the need for data communications services has grown, it has become necessary to connect networks together for the sharing of resources and distribution of functions and for administrative control. In addition, some LANs, by virtue of their restricted distance, often need to be connected together through other de-

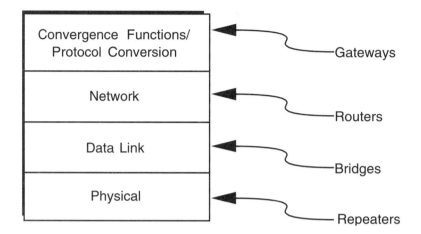

Figure A–7   Placement of internetworking units.

vices. These devices are called a number of names in the industry; in this section we will explain and define each of these machines.

Figure A–7 shows the relationships of these devices vis-à-vis a layered model. A *repeater* is used to connect the media on a LAN, typically called media segments. The repeater has no upper layer functions, its principal job is to terminate the signal on one LAN segment and regenerate it on another LAN segment. The repeater is not an internetworking unit (IWU).

The term *bridge* is usually associated with an IWU. It operates at the data link layer. Typically, it uses a 48-bit media access control (MAC) address to perform its relaying functions. As a general rule, it is a fairly low-function device and connects networks that are homogeneous (for example, IEEE-based local area networks [LANs]).

A *router* operates at the network layer because it uses network layer addresses (for example, IP, X.121, E.164 addresses). It usually contains more capabilities than a bridge and may offer flow control mechanisms as well as source routing or nonsource routing features.

The term *gateway* is used to describe an entity (a machine or software module) that not only performs routing capabilities but may act as a protocol conversion or mapping facility (also called a convergence function). For example, such a gateway could relay traffic and also provide conversion between two different types of mail transfer applications.

Yet another term that has entered the market is the term *brouter,* which is used to describe a machine that combines the features of a router and a bridge. This somewhat artificial term is falling into disuse in the industry.

To avoid any confusion about these terms, some people use the term *internetworking unit (IWU)*. An IWU is a generic term to describe a router, a gateway, a bridge, or anything else that performs relaying functions between networks. Several standards groups use the term interworking unit in place of internetworking unit.

Bridges are designed to interconnect LANs; therefore, it is convenient for them to use a MAC address in determining how to relay the traffic between LANs. Additionally, a bridge "pushes" the conventional network layer responsibilities of route discovery and relaying operations into the data link layer. In effect, a bridge has no conventional network layer.

By virtue of the design of a bridge (no technical reason exists why a bridge could not exhibit more functionality), it has relatively limited capabilities. On the other hand, bridges are fast and they are easy to implement. Indeed, most bridges are self-configuring. This feature relieves network managers of many onerous tasks, such as constant management of a number of naming and network reconfiguration parameters.

Routers can use the same type of route discovery and relay operations as a bridge. Indeed, many routers and bridges use the same type of operation to determine how to route traffic to the next network. As examples, minimum hop operations and link state routing can be used at either the data link or the network layer.

Therefore, other than addressing, what is the difference between a router and a bridge and why should there be options to use one or the other? A bridge is designed for fewer functions than a conventional router. A router typically allows multiple network protocols to run on the machine. As examples, AppleTalk, DECnet IV, IP, and IPX are commonly supported in routers. In contrast, since a bridge does not use the network layer, it does not have these components. Multiprotocol traffic can certainly pass through the bridge, but the bridge is unaware of these operations; its job is to examine the MAC address in the frame and relay the frame to the next node (bridge or user device). Finally, LAN bridges use broadcasting in many of their operations; that is, the traffic is sent to *all* stations on a network (or networks).

Additionally, bridges have been designed to support the internetworking of LANs only. Consequently, the use of a MAC layer and the MAC relay entity is consistent with LAN architecture. The MAC relay entity can be implemented in hardware, which makes bridge operations efficient and fast.

In contrast, routers are usually implemented with software and provide more extensive value-added features than bridges. Their software orientation makes them more flexible that bridges. Additionally, routers use a layer three address, such as IP, which is designed to support hierarchical routing and is more efficient than the MAC address, which is a flat (nonhierarchical) address. Routers can also route based on TOS/QOS. For example, a field in the PDU may stipulate a certain priority for the traffic and the router can treat the PDU accordingly. This feature will become increasingly important as routers integrate ATM into their architectures, which is the subject of much of this book.

Appendix **B**

Addressing Conventions

INTRODUCTION

This appendix provides a review of addressing conventions, and concentrates on the addresses used by the technologies covered in this book: (a) IEEE 802 MAC addresses, (b) IP addresses and (c) ATM addresses.

THE MAC ADDRESS

The IEEE assigns universal LAN physical addresses and universal protocol identifiers. Previously this work was performed by the Xerox Corporation by administering what were known as block identifiers (Block IDs) for Ethernet addresses. Previously, the Xerox Ethernet Administration Office assigned these values, which were three octets (24 bits) in length. The organization that received this address was free to use the remaining 24 bits of the Ethernet address in any way it chose.

Due to the progress made in the IEEE 802 project, it was decided that the IEEE would assume the task of assigning these universal identifiers for all LANs, not just CSMA/CD types of networks. However, the IEEE continues to honor the assignments made by the Ethernet administration office although it now calls the block ID an *organization unique identifier (OUI)*.

The format for the OUI is shown in Figure B–1. The least significant bit of the address space corresponds to the individual/group (I/G) address bit. The I/G address bit, if set to a zero, means that the address field identifies an individual address. If the value is set to a one, the address field identifies a group address which is used to identify more than one station connected to the LAN. If the entire OUI is set to all ones, it signifies a broadcast address which identifies all stations on the network.

The second bit of the address space is the local or universal bit (U/L). When this bit is set to a zero, it has universal assignment significance–for example, from the IEEE. If it is set to a one it is an address that is locally assigned. Bit position number two must always be set to a zero if it is administered by the IEEE.

The OUI is extended to include a 48 bit universal LAN address (which is designated as the *media access control [MAC]* address). The 24 bits of the address space is the same as the OUI assigned by the IEEE. The one exception is that the I/G bit may be set to a one or a zero to identify group or individual addresses. The second part of the address space consisting of the remaining 24 bits is locally administered and can be set to any values an organization chooses.

Is the 48 bit address space sufficient for the future? 48 bits provide for a 2^{48} value, which can identify about 281.475 trillion unique addresses, so it should be sufficient for a while.

Each OUI gives an organization the 24-bit address space (which is quite large), although the true address space is 22 bits because the first

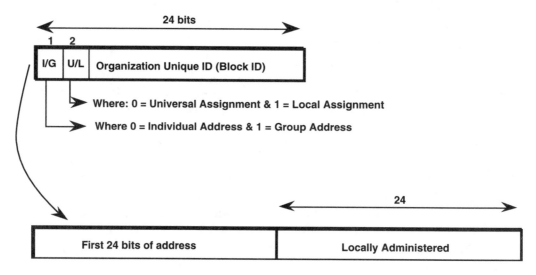

Figure B–1   The MAC address.

two bits are used for control, and administrative purposes. This means that the address space is 2^{22}.

The second part of the address space consisting of the remaining 24 bits is locally administered and can be set to any values an organization chooses. This part of the address is shown in the figure as "Locally Administered".

THE IP ADDRESS

Internet networks use a 32-bit address to identify a host computer and the network to which the host is attached. The structure of the IP address is depicted in Figure B–2. Its format is:

IP Address = Network Address + Host Address

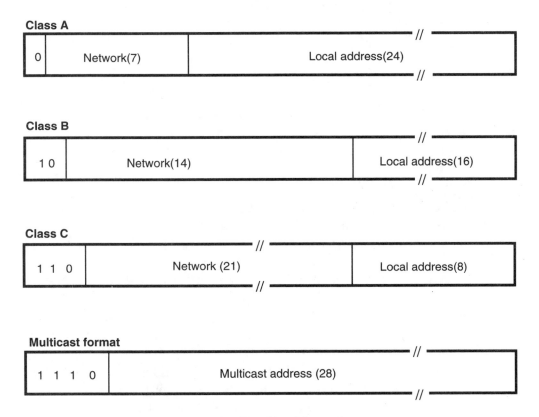

Figure B–2   The IP address format.

IP addresses are classified by their formats. Four formats are permitted: class A, class B, class C, or class D formats. The first bits of the address specify the format of the remainder of the address field in relation to the network and host subfields. The host address is also called the local address.

The *class A* addresses provide for networks that have a large number of hosts. The host ID field is 24 bits. Therefore, 2^{24} hosts can be identified. Seven bits are devoted to the network ID, which supports an identification scheme for as many as 127 networks (bit values of 1 to 127).

Class B addresses are used for networks of intermediate size. Fourteen bits are assigned for the network ID, and 16 bits are assigned for the host ID. *Class C* networks contain fewer than 256 hosts (2^8). Twenty-one bits are assigned to the network ID. Finally, *class D* addresses are reserved for multicasting, which is a form of broadcasting but within a limited area.

For ease in reading, the IP address is depicted in a decimal form of X.X.X.X, where each X represents an eight-bit byte. For example, an IP address can appear as 172.16.17.88.

THE OSI ADDRESS FORMAT

ISO 7498 3 and X.213 (Annex A) describe a hierarchical structure for the network service access point (NSAP) address, and ISO 8348/DAD 2 (Draft Addendum 2) specifies the structure for the NSAP address. It consists of four parts, shown in Figure B–3:

- *Initial Domain Part* (IDP): Contains the authority format identifier (AFI) and the initial domain identifier (IDI).
- *Authority Format Identifier* (AFI): Contains a two-digit value between 0 and 99. It is used to identify (a) the IDI format, the authority responsible for the IDI values, and (b) the syntax of the domain specific part (DSP).
- *Initial Domain Identifier* (IDI): Specifies the addressing domain and the network addressing authority for the DSP values. It is interpreted according to the AFI.
- *Domain Specific Part* (DSP): Contains the address determined by the network authority. It is an address below the second level of the addressing hierarchy. It can contain addresses of user end systems on an individual subnetwork.

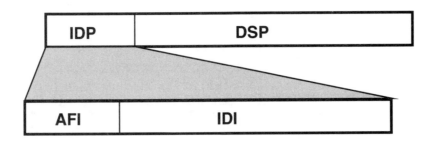

where:
IDP   Initial domain part
AFI   Authority format identifier
IDI   Initial domain identifier
DSP   Domain specific Part
And Where for AFI
00-99   Reserved-will not be allocated
10-35   Reserved for future allocation
36-59   Allocated by ITU-T and ISO
60-69   For new IDI formats, assigned by ISO
70-79   For new IDI formats, assigned by ITU-T
80-99   Reserved for future allocation

Figure B–3   The OSI address.

ATM ADDRESS FORMAT

Figure B–4 shows an example of the OSI addressing scheme, as used by the Asynchronous Transfer Mode (ATM). The ATM address is modeled on the OSI network service access point (NSAP), and is coded as follows:

1. The Initial *Domain Part* (IDP): Contains the authority format identifier (AFI) and the initial domain identifier (IDI), described earlier.
2. The *Authority Format Identifier* (AFI): Identifies the specific part (DSP). For ATM, AFI field is coded as:
   39 = DCC ATM format
   47 = ICD ATM format
   45 = E.164 format
3. *Initial Domain Identifier* (IDI): It is interpreted according to the AFI (where AFI = 39, 47, or 45). For ATM, the IDI is coded as (a)

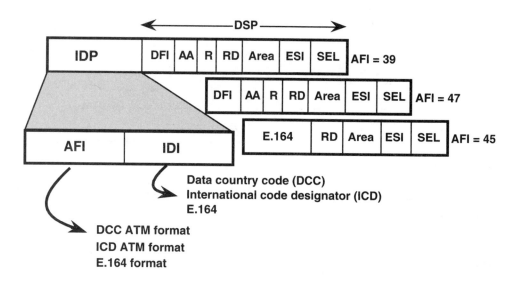

Figure B–4   The ATM address format.

a data country code (DCC), in accordance with ISO 3166, (b) an international code designator (ICD), which identifies an international organization, and is maintained by the British Standards Institute, or (c) an E.164 address, which is a telephone number.

4. The *Domain Specific Part* (DSP): For ATM, the contents vary, depending on value of the AFI. The domain specific part identifier (DFI), specifies the syntax and other aspects of the remainder of the DSP. The administrative authority (AA) is an organization assigned by the ISO that is responsible for the allocation of values in certain fields in the DSP. The R field is a reserved field.

The routing domain identifier (RD) specifies a domain that must be unique within either: (a) for AFI = 39, DCC/DFI/AA; (b) for AFI = 47, ICD/DFI/AA, and (c) for AFI = 45, E.164. The area identifies a unique area within a routing domain, and the end system identifier (ESI) identifies an end system (such as a computer) within the area.

The selector (SEL) is not used by an ATM network. It usually identifies the protocol entities in the upper layers of the user machine that are to receive the traffic. Therefore, the SEL could contain upper layer SAPs.

ATM public networks must support the E.164 address and private networks must support all formats.

Appendix C

LANE Parameters

The following parameters are part of the LANE specifications, and are cited in the LANE chapters.

C1   **LE Client's ATM Addresses.** The LE Client's own ATM Addresses.

C2   **LAN Type.** The type of LAN of which that the LE Client is, Ethernet/IEEE 802.3, IEEE 802.5, or Unspecified.

C3   **Maximum Data Frame Size.** The maximum AAL-5 SDU size of a data frame that the LE Client wishes to send on the Multicast Send VCC or to receive on the Multicast Send VCC or Multicast Forward VCC.

C4   **Proxy.** Indicates whether the LE Client may have remote unicast MAC addresses in C27.

C5   **ELAN Name.** The identity of the emulated LAN the LE Client.

C6   **Local Unicast MAC Address(es).** Each LE Client has zero or more local unicast MAC addresses.

C7   **Control Time-out.** Used for timing out most request/response control frame interactions.

> Value: Minimum = 10 seconds, Default = 120 seconds, Maximum = 300 seconds.

C8   **Route Descriptor(s).** Used for source-routed IEEE 802.5 LE Clients that are Source-Route Bridges.

C9   **LE Server ATM Address.** The ATM address of the LAN Emulation Server is used to establish the Control Direct VCC.

C10   **Maximum Unknown Frame Count.**
Value: Minimum = 1, Default = 1, Maximum = 10. (See parameter C11.)

C11   **Maximum Unknown Frame Time.** Within the period of time defined by the Maximum Unknown Frame Time, an LE Client will send no more than Maximum Unknown Frame Count frames to the BUS for a given unicast LAN Destination.
Value: Minimum = 1 second, Default = 1 second, Maximum = 60 seconds.

C12   **VCC Time-out Period.** To release any Data Direct VCC that LEC has not been used to transmit or receive any data frames for the length of the VCC Time-out Period.
Value: Minimum = None specified, Default = 20 minutes, Maximum = Unlimited.

C13   **Maximum Retry Count.** An LE Client MUST not retry an LE_ARP_REQUEST for a given frame's LAN destination more than Maximum Retry Count times, after the first LE_ARP_REQUEST for that same frame's LAN destination.
Value: Minimum = 0, Default = 1, Maximum = 2.

C14   **LE Client Identifier.** Each LE Client has an LE Client Identifier (LECID) assigned by the LE Server during the Join phase.

C15   **LE Client Multicast MAC Address(es).** A list of multicast MAC addresses which the LEC wishes to receive and pass up to the higher layers.

C16   **LE_ARP Cache.** A table of entries, each of which establishes a relationship between a LAN Destination external to the LE Client and the ATM address to which data frames for the LAN Destination will be sent.

C17   **Aging Time.** The maximum time that an LE Client will maintain an entry in its LE_ARP cache in the absence of a verification of that relationship.
Value: Minimum = 10 seconds, Default = 300 seconds, Maximum = 300 seconds.

C18   **Forward Delay Time.** The maximum time that an LE Client will maintain an entry for a non-local MAC address in its LE_ARP cache in the absence of a verification of that relationship, as long as the Topology Change flag C19 is true.

Value[16]: Minimum = 4 seconds, Default = 15 seconds, Maximum = 30 seconds.

C19   **Topology Change.** Indication that the LE Client is using the Forward Delay Time C18, instead of the Aging Time C17, to age non-local entries in its LE_ARP cache C16.

C20   **Expected LE_ARP Response Time.** The maximum time that the LEC expects an LE_ARP_REQUEST/LE_ARP_RE-SPONSE cycle to take.

Value: Minimum = 1 second, Default = 1 second, Maximum = 30 seconds.

C21   **Flush Time-out.** Time limit to wait to receive an LE_FLUSH_RESPONSE after the LE_FLUSH_REQUEST has been sent before taking recovery action.

Value: Minimum = 1 second, Default = 4 seconds, Maximum = 4 seconds.

C22   **Path Switching Delay.** The time since sending a frame to the BUS after which the LE Client may assume that the frame has been either discarded or delivered to the recipient.

Value: Minimum = 1 second, Default = 6 seconds, Maximum = 8 seconds.

C23   **Local Segment ID.** The segment ID of the emulated LAN.

C24   **Multicast Send VCC Type.** Signaling parameter used by the LE Client when establishing the Multicast Send VCC.

C25   **Multicast Send VCC AvgRate.** Signaling parameter used by the LE Client when establishing the Multicast Send VCC.

C26   **Multicast Send VCC PeakRate.** Signaling parameter used by the LE Client when establishing the Multicast Send VCC.

C27   **Remote Unicast MAC Address(es).** The MAC addresses for which this LE Client will answer LE_ARP_REQUESTs, but which are not registered with the LE Server.

C28   **Connection Completion Timer.** In Connection Establishment this is the time period in which data or a READY_IND message is expected from a Calling Party.

Value: Minimum = 1 second, Default = 4 seconds, Maximum = 10 seconds.

REVIEW 1

X.25 and Related Protocols

1. Summarize the main functions of X.25.

2. Answer true or false.
   a. X.25 is a packet-switching protocol.   T   F
   b. X.25 defines the network interface with the user. T   F
   c. X.25 defines the internal network operations.   T   F
   d. X.25 is a connectionless protocol.   T   F
3. Contrast connectionless and connection-oriented protocols.

4. Can a network exhibit both connectionless and connection-oriented characteristics? Explain why or why not.

5. What are the differences between logical channels and virtual circuits?

6. Briefly describe the functions of the X.25 layers.

Abbreviations

AAL CP: AAL common part
AAL5: ATM adaptation layer, type 5
ACL: Automatic congestion level
AESA: ATM end system address
ARP: Address Resolution Protocol
AA: Administrative authority
AAL: ATM adaptation layer
ACCS: Automated calling card service
ACM: Address complete message
AE: Application entity
AEI: Application entity invocation
AFI: Authority format identifier
AIS: Alarm indication signal
AP: Applications process
ASE: Application service element
ATM: Asynchronous Transfer Mode
B-ISDN: Broadband-ISDN
B-ISUP: Broadband-ISDN user part
BC: Bearer capability
BCC: Bearer connection control
BER: Basic encoding rules
BGAK: Begin acknowledge
BGN: Begin
BGRE: Begin reject
BOM: Beginning of message
BR: Buffer release
BRI: Basic rate interface

BSS: Broadband Switching System
C: Cell loss priority
CAC: Connection admission control
CBR: Constant bit rate
CC: Call control
CC: Country code
CCIS: Common channel interoffice signaling
CCRI: Consistency check result information
CCITT: International Telecommunications Union-Telecommunication Standardization Sector (see also ITU-T)
CCS: Common channel signaling
CCS I/F: CCS interface
CMIP: Common management information protocol
COM: Continuation of message
CPCS: Common part convergence sublayer
CPCS: Common part CS
CPCS-UU: Common part convergence sublayer-user-to-user
CPE: Customer premises equipment
CPI: Common part id
CPI: Common part indicator
CRC: Cyclic redundancy check
CS: Convergence sublayer

CUG: Closed user group
DCC: Data country code
DN: Destination network
DPC: Destination point code
DSAP: Destination SAP
DSID: Destination signaling identifier
DSP: Domain specific part
DSS: Digital subscriber signaling system
ENDAK: End acknowledge
E800: Enhanced 800
EOM: End of message
ER: Error recovery
ERAK: Error recovery acknowledge
ESI: End system identifier
FEC: Forward error correction
FERF: Far End Receive Failure
FOT: Forward transfer message
GFC: Generic flow control
GSM: Global systems for mobile communications
GT: Global title
HEC: Header error check
HEC: Header error control
HO DSP: High order domain specific part
IAA: IAM acknowledgment
IAM: Initial address
IC: Interchange carrier
ICD: International code designator
ICI: Intercarrier interface
ID: Interface data
id: Identification
IDI: Initial domain identifier
IDP: Initial domain part
IE: Information elements
IP: Internet Protocol
IPI: Initial protocol identifier
ISDN: Integrated Services Digital Network
ISUP: ISDN user part
IT: Information type
ITU-T: International Telecommunications Union-Telecommunication Standardization Sector (ITU-T, formerly, the CCITT)
IXC: Interchange carrier
LCN: Logical channel number
LE: List element
LEC: Local exchange carrier
LI: Length indicator
LLC: Logical link control

LLC: Low layer compatibility
LM: Layer management
LMI: Local management interface
MC: Maintenance control
MCI: Message compatibility information
MD: Management data
MID: Message id
MTP 3: Message transfer part 3
MTP: Message transfer part
MU: Message unit
MUSN: MU sequence number
N-BC: Narrowband bearer capability
N-HLC: Narrowband high layer capability
N-ISDN: Narrowband Integrated Services Digital Network
NLPID: Network level PID
N-LLC: Narrowband low layer compatibility
NDC: National destination code
NNI: Network-node interface
NNI: Network-to-network interface
NSAP: Network service access point
N(S)N: National (significant) number
OSI Model: Open Systems Interconnection Model
OAM: Operations, administration, and maintenance
OUI: Organization unique ID
OPC: Originating point code
OSID: Origination signaling identifier
PAD: Padding
PBX: Private branch exchange
PC: Point code
PCI: Protocol control information
PCM: Pulse code modulation
PCR: Peak cell rate
PCS: Personal communications services
PDU: Protocol data unit
PHY: Physical layer
PID: Protocol id
PL: Physical layer
PM: Physical medium sublayer
PRI: Primary rate interface
PTI: Payload type identifier
PTO: Public telecommunications operators
PVC: Permanent virtual circuit
QOS: Quality of service
REL: Release
RES: Resume

RJE: Remote job entry

RLC: Release complete

ROSE: Remote operations service element

SAAL: Signaling ATM adaptation layer

SACF: Single association control function

SAO: Single association object

SAP: Service access point

SAR: Segmentation and reassembly

SCCP: Signaling connection control point

SCP: Service control point

SD: Sequenced data

SDU: Service data unit

SE: Status enquiry

SEL: Selector

SID: Signaling identifier

SIO: Service information octet

SLS: Signaling link selection code

SN: Sequence number

SN: Subscriber's number

SNAP: Subnetwork access protocol

SNMP: Simple Network Management Protocol

SNP: Sequence number protection

SONET: Synchronous Optical Network

SP: Signaling point

SPF: Shortest path first

SS7: Signaling System Number 7

SSAP: Source service access point

SSCF: Service-specific coordination function

SSCOP: Service-specific connection-oriented protocol

SSCOP-UU: SSCOP user-to-user

SSCS LM: Service specific convergence sublayer layer management

SSCS: Service specific convergence sublayer

SSM: Single segment message

SSN: Subsystem number

SSP: Service switching point

STAT: Solicited status response

STP: Signaling transfer point

SUS: Suspend message

SVC: Switched virtual call or channel

TA: Terminal adapter

TCAP: Transaction capabilities application part

TC: Transmission convergence sublayer

TC: Trunk code

TCP/IP: Transmission central protocol/Internet protocol

TDM: Time division multiplexing

TUP: Telephone user part

UD: Unnumbered data

UI: Unrecognized information

ULP: Upper layer protocol

UNI: User-network interface

USTAT: Unsolicited status

VBR: Variable bit rate

VC: Virtual channel

VCC: Virtual channel connection

VCI: Virtual channel identifier

VCI: Virtual circuit identifier

VPC: Virtual path connection

VPCI: Virtual path connection identifier

VPI: Virtual path identifier

VPN: Virtual private network

Other References

In addition to the formal standards for the systems described in this book, these references should prove useful to the reader. Many of them were used for the development of this material.

[AHMA93] Amhad, R., and Halsall, F. (1993). Interconnecting high-speed LANs and backbones, *IEEE Network*, September.

[AMOS79] Amos, J.E., Jr. (1979). Circuit switching: Unique architecture and applications. *IEEE Computer*, June.

[ARMT93] Armitage, G.J., and Adams, K.M.(1993). Packet reassembly during cell loss, *IEEE Network*, September.

[ATM92a] ATM Forum. (June 1, 1992). *ATM user-network interface specification, Version 2.0.*

[ATM93a] ATM Forum. (August 5, 1993). *ATM user-network interface specification, Version 3.0.*

[ATM94a] ATM Forum. (March, 1994). *Education and training work group*, ATM Forum Ambassador's Program.

[ATM94b] ATM Forum. (July 21, 1994). *ATM user-network interface specification, Version 3.1.*

[ATT89a] (January, 1989). Observations of error characteristics of fiber optic transmission systems, CCITT SGXVIII, San Diego, CA.

[BELL82] Bellamy, J. (1982). *Digital Telephony*, New York, NY: John Wiley and Sons.

[BELL90a] (May, 1993). Generic requirements for frame relay PVC exchange service, TR-TSV-001369, Issue 1.

[BELL89a]. (September, 1989). Synchronous optical network (SONET) transport systems: common generic criteria, TR-TSY-000253, Issue 1.

[BELL94] Bellman, R.B. (1994). Evolving traditional LANs to ATM, *Business Communications Review*, October.

[BLAC89] Black, U. (1989). *Data Networks, Concepts, Theory and Practice*, Prentice Hall.

[BLAC91] Black, U. (1991). *X.25 and related protocols*, IEEE Computer Society Press.

[BLAC93] Black, U. (1993). *Data link protocols*, Prentice Hall.

[BLAI88] Blair, C. (1988). SLIPs: Definitions, causes, and effects in T1 networks, *A Tautron Application Note, Issue 1*, September. (Note: my thanks to this author for a lucid explanation of slips.)

[BNR92a] Bell Northern Research. (1992). Global systems for mobile communications, *Telesis*, 92.

[BNR94a] Discussions held with Bell Northern Research (BNR) designers during 1993 and 1994.

[BROW94] Brown, P.D. (ed.). (1994). The price is right for ATM to become a serious competitor, *Broadband Networking News*, May.

[CCIT90a] (1990). Voice packetization-packetized voice protocols, CCITT Recommendation G.764, Geneva.

[CDPD93] (July 19, 1993). Cellular digital packet data system specification, *Release 1.0*.

[CHER92] Cherukuri, R. (August 26, 1992). Voice over frame relay networks, A technical paper issued as Frame Relay Forum, FRF 92.33.

[CHEU92] Cheung, N.K. (1992). The infrastructure of gigabit computer networks, *IEEE Communications Magazine*, April,.

[COMM94a] Korostoff, K. (April 18, 1994). Wide-area ATM undergoes trial by MAGIC, *Communications Week*.

[DAVI91] Davidson, R.P., and Muller, N.J. (1991). *The Guide to SONET*, Telecom Library, Inc.

[DELL92] Dell Computer, Intel, and University of Pennsylvania, A study compiled by Marty Baumann, *USA Today*, date not available.

[dePr91] dePrycker, M. (1991). *Asynchronous Transfer Mode*. Ellis Harwood Ltd.

[dePR92] de Prycker, M. (1992) ATM in Belgian Trial. *Communications International*, June.

[DUBO94] DuBois, D. Simnet Inc., Palo Alto, CA. A recommendation from a reviewer of *Emerging Communications Technologies*. (Thank you Mr. DuBois.)

[ECKB92] Eckberg, A.E. (1992). B-ISDN/ATM traffic and congestion control, *IEEE Network*, September.

[EMLI 63] Emling, J.W., and Mitchell, D. (1963). The effects of time delay and echoes on telephone conversations. *Bell Systems Technical Journal*, November.

[FORD93] Ford, P.S., Rekhter, Y., and Braun, H.-W. (1993). Improving the routing and addressing of IP. *IEEE Network*, May.

[FORU92] Frame Relay Forum Technical Committee. (May 7, 1992). "Frame relay network-to-network interface, phase 1 implementation agreement, Document Number FRF 92.08R1–Draft 1.4.

[GASM93] Gasman, L. (1993). ATM CPE—Who is providing what?, *Business Communications Review*, October.

[GOKE73] Goke, L.R., and Lipovski, G.J. (1973). Banyan networks for partitioning multiprocessor systems. First Annual Symposium on Computer Architecture.

[GRIL93] Grillo, D., MacNamee, R.J.G., and Rashidzadeh, B. (1993). Towards third generation mobile systems: A European possible transition path. *Computer Networks and ISDN Systems*, 25(8).

[GRON92] Gronert, E. (1992). MANS make their mark in Germany. *Data Communications International*, May.

[HAFN94] Hafner, K. (1994). Making sense of the internet. *Newsweek*, October 24.

[HALL92] Hall, M. (ed.). (1992). LAN-based ATM products ready to roll out. *LAN Technology*, September.

[HAND91] Handel, R., and Huber, M.N. (1991). *Integrated broadband networks: An introduction to ATM-based networks*. Addison-Wesley.

[HERM93] Herman, J., and Serjak C. (1993). ATM switches and hubs lead the way to a new era of switched internetworks. *Data Communications*, March.

[HEWL91] Hewlett Packard, Inc. (1991). Introduction to SONET, A tutorial.

[HEWL92] Hewlett Packard, Inc. (1992). Introduction to SONET networks and tests, An internal document.

[HEYW93] Heywood, P. (1993). PTTs gear up to offer high-speed services. *Data Communications*, August.

[HILL91] SONET, An overview. A paper prepared by Hill Associates, Inc., Winooski, VT, 05404.

[HUNT92] Hunter, P. (1992). What price progress?, *Communications International*, June.

[ITU93a] ITU-TS (1993). ITU-TS draft recommendation Q93.B "B-ISDN user-network interface layer 3 specification for basic call/bearer control. May.

[JAYA81] Jayant, N.S., and Christensen, S.W. (1981). Effects of packet losses on waveform-coded speech and improvements due to an odd-even interpolation procedure. *IEEE Transactions of Communications*, February.

[JOHN91] Johnson, J.T. (1991). Frame relay mux meets cell relay switch. *Data Communications*, October.

[JOHN92] Johnson, J.T. (1992). "Getting access to ATM. *Data Communications LAN Interconnect*, September 21.

[KING94] King, S.S. (1994). Switched virtual networks. *Data Communications*, September.

[KITA91] Kitawaki, N., and Itoh, K. (1991). Pure delay effects of speech quality in telecommunications. *IEEE Journal of Selected Areas in Communications*, May.

[LEE89] Lee, W.C.Y. (1989). *Mobile cellular telecommunications systems*. McGraw-Hill.

[LEE93] Lee, B.G., Kang, M., and Lee, J. (1993). *Broadband telecommunications technology*. Artech House.

[LISO91] Lisowski, B. (1991). Frame relay: what it is and how it works. *A Guide to Frame Relay, Supplement to Business Communications Review*, October.

[LIZZ94] Lizzio, J.R. (1994). Real-time RAID stokrage: the enabling technology for video-on-demand. *Telephony*, May 23.

[LYLE92] Lyles, J.B., and Swinehart, D.C. (1992). The emerging gigabit environment and the role of the local ATM. *IEEE Communications Magazine*, April.

[McCO94] McCoy, E. (1994). SONET, ATM and other broadband technologies. TRA Document # ATL72 16.9100, *Telecommunications Research Associates*, St. Marys, KS.

[MCQU91] McQuillan, J.M. (1991). Cell relay switching. *Data Communications*, September.

[MINO93] Minoli D. (1993). Proposed Cell Relay Bearer Service Stage 1 Description, T1S1.1/93-136 (Revision 1), ANSI Committee T1 (T1S1.1), June.

[MORE9] Moreney, J. (1994). ATM switch decision can wait, *Network World*, September 19.

[NOLL91] Nolle, T. (1991). Frame relay: Standards advance, *Business Communications Review*, October.

[NORT94] Northern Telecom. (1994). Consultant Bulletin 63020.16/02-94, Issue 1, February.

[[NYQU24] Nyquist, H. (1924). Certain factors affecting telegraph speed. *Transactions A.I.E.E.*

[PERL85] Perlman, R. (1985). An algorithm for distributed computation of spanning tree in an extended LAN. *Computer Communications Review*, *15*(4) September.

[ROSE92] Rosenberry, W., Kenney D., and Fisher, G. (1992). *Understanding DCE*. O'Reilly & Associates.

[SALA92] Salamone, S. (1992). Sizing up the most critical issues. *Network World*.

[SAND94] Sandberg, J. (1994). Networking. *Wall Street Journal*, November 14.

[SHAN48] Shannon, C. (1948). Mathematical theory of communication, *Bell System Technical Journal, 27*, July and October.

[SRIR90a] Sriram, K. (1990a). Dynamic bandwidth allocation and congestion control schemes for voice and data integration in wideband packet technology, *Proc. IEEE. Supercomm/ICC '90, 3*, April.

[SRIR90b] Sriram, K. (1990b). Bandwidth allocation and congestion control scheme for an integrated voice and data network. *US Patent No. 4, 914650*, April 3.

[SRIR93a] Sriram, K. (1993). Methodologies for bandwidth allocation, transmission scheduling, and congestion avoidance in broadband ATM networks. *Computer Networks and ISDN Systems*, *26*(1), September.

[SRIR93b] Sriram, K., and Lucantoni, D.M. (1993). Traffic smoothing effects of bit dropping in a packet voice multiplexer. *IEEE Transactions on Communications*, July.

[STEW92] Steward, S.P. (1992). The world report '92. *Cellular Business*, May.

[WADA89] Wada, M. (1989). Selective recovery of video packet loss using error concelment. *IEEE Journal of Selected Areas in Communications*, June.

[WALL91] Wallace, B. (1991). Citicorp goes SONET. *Network World*, November 18.

[WERK92] Wernik, M., Aboul-Magd, O., and Gilber, H. (1992). Traffic management for B-ISDN services. *IEEE Network*, September.

[WEST92] Westgate, J. (1992).*OSI Management*, NCC Blackwell.

[WILL92] Williamson, J. (1992). GSM bids for global recognition in a crowded cellular world. *Telephony*, April 6.

[WU93] Wu, T.-H. (1993). Cost-effective network evolution. *IEEE Communications Magazine*, September.

[YAP93] Yap, M.-T., and Hutchison (1993). An emulator for evaluating DQDB performance. *Computer Networks and ISDN Systems*, *25*(11).

[YOKO93] Yokotani, T., Sato, H., and Nakatsuka, S. (1993). A study on a performance improvement algorithm in DQDB MAN. *Computer Networks and ISDN Systems*, *25*(10).

Index